NO TIME TO QUIT

Life in a
Broken Package

Gail Lipe

WESTBOW
PRESS
A DIVISION OF THOMAS NELSON

WestBow Press books may be ordered through booksellers or by contacting:

WestBow Press
A Division of Thomas Nelson
1663 Liberty Drive
Bloomington, IN 47403
www.westbowpress.com
1-(866) 928-1240

Because of the dynamic nature of the Internet, any web addresses or links contained in this book may have changed since publication and may no longer be valid. The views expressed in this work are solely those of the author and do not necessarily reflect the views of the publisher, and the publisher hereby disclaims any responsibility for them.

Any people depicted in stock imagery provided by Thinkstock are models, and such images are being used for illustrative purposes only.

Certain stock imagery © Thinkstock.

ISBN: 978-1-4908-0096-7 (sc)
ISBN: 978-1-4908-0098-1 (hc)
ISBN: 978-1-4908-0097-4 (e)

Library of Congress Control Number: 2013912226

Printed in the United States of America.

WestBow Press rev. date: 7/15/2013

This book is dedicated to my mother.

I would like to thank Lee Ostrom for helping edit this book and believing in the importance of its story, and my daughter, Joy, and husband, Stephen, for helping make this book a reality.

FORWARD

First, know that Gail Lipe is a God-fearing woman.

Kind, genuine and that someone who sees a half-full glass, she flashes one of the more magnificent smiles one will ever encounter.

Gail and I came to know each other while working long hours during the first decade of the 21st century at The Chronicle newspaper in Glencoe, Minn. We were reporters.

I recall that we laughed hearty laughs, discussed religions, politics and journalism with a gusto, and more than anything else, kept current on our families.

Family is dear to Gail, who for years said she would write down her mother's remarkable life story and have it published. Now, she has done just that.

No Time to Quit is an up-close report about a woman, diagnosed with cerebral palsy at birth, confounding doctors not only with her longevity, but also the quality of her amazing life.

If you do not shed tears while reading *No Time to Quit*, you are more hardened than I. Either way, you are certain to be inspired.

—Lee Ostrom,
newspaper reporter, photographer,
and editor for more than 30 years.

INTRODUCTION

Everyone has a story.

My years as a journalist taught me that. What seems ordinary to the subject of the story may be an amazing inspiration to someone else. The everyday life of one person can sometimes validate another's existence, or give someone the feeling that he is not alone.

Some people's stories are filled with miracles that leave no room for questions about the existence of God. They give hope. My mother's story is one of those. Though she has known no other way of life her persistence, perseverance, and strength throughout her lifetime have touched the lives of others. She never let cerebral palsy dictate her existence.

Cerebral palsy is an injury to the motor area of the brain similar to an aneurism or stroke. The cause itself can be bleeding in the brain, lack of oxygen to the brain, or something that interferes with the development of the brain.

My mother's injury happened at birth, and she was blessed with parents whose thoughts on handicapped children were way ahead of their time. It was common in the 1930s to hide those with handicaps, but when others suggested my mother be put in an institution, her parents refused. Her mother knew there was more inside that little blonde-haired, blue-eyed head than was suggested by the garbled noises coming out of her mouth.

My mother's parents also had the empowering wisdom that allowed Mom to make many of the major decisions about her life, even at a young age. Instead of assuming Mom could not do things, they enabled her to take on difficult tasks and encouraged her to challenge herself.

There also were circumstances some people would call coincidences that helped change and shape my mother's life. I call them miracles.

All aspects of life are created by the balance of a series of decisions, and some of those decisions affect more than we will ever know. With some decisions, we can clearly see the miracles that are produced; with others, the outcomes remain obscure. It may appear that a specific decision will not affect anything one way or the other, and then something life-changing happens.

My mother calls those incidents divine intervention. They are often an answer to many prayers.

Mom's life is littered with miracles that came from decisions made by strong, passionate people. She has been surrounded by love from before she was born, and that love pushed her and sustained her through the many challenges she has faced. It also gave her a strong sense of perseverance.

Even now, in her 80s, Mom continues to shine through her broken package. She astounds people with the way she does everyday things able-bodied people take for granted. Things as simple as getting dressed, or getting into bed. Though accomplishing daily routines is harder and takes longer as she gets older, she continues to find ways to adapt to the challenges.

This book is a gift. It tells the story of one family overcoming seemingly unbeatable odds, a story filled with heaven-orchestrated coincidences that helped shape the woman who gave birth to me. I hope it brings inspiration to those who read it, and that they come to understand that there really is no time to quit.

CHAPTER 1

—⁂—

The Beginning

"Wayne, we've got to go! Something's wrong!"

Lillie, barely twenty years old, knew at six months pregnant it was way too early to give birth to her first child, but she was bleeding. The chances of a premature baby surviving in 1932 were remote. They needed to get to a hospital.

Worried about his wife and baby, Wayne took Lillie to the closest hospital, a small ten-bed facility established in an old farmhouse about ten miles away in the city of Norwich, Kansas. Lillie's doctor (and the hospital's founder) Eugene Wallace was not there. He was about forty miles away at the osteopathic hospital in Wichita.

As the bleeding continued to get worse, Dr. Wallace was called. He told the couple to stay put. He would be there as soon as he could.

When the doctor arrived, concern was written all over his face. There was no way to stop the birth, so Lillie was taken to the operating room. Wayne was sent to wait on a porch, where all he could do was pace, pray and hope.

The afterbirth came first, and the prognosis was not good for either mother or child.

"If we don't do something immediately, we will lose them both," said Dr. Wallace. The decision was made to perform an emergency cesarean section in an effort to at least save Lillie.

The thought of losing Lillie was unbearable. As Wayne looked back, he could see her in the pale blue dress she wore when they were married the summer before, and he recounted the precious moments they had spent together.

Wayne's reputation of being a wild young man preceded him, though the reputation was not quite accurate. It was intentionally constructed by his mischievous behavior, sense of humor, and lack of care for what other people thought. The antics he and his best friend performed included slipping vanilla bottles into their back pockets while walking down Main Street being loud and obnoxious, giving people the impression they were drunk. When they were sure their performance gained the appropriate attention, they would hide out at one or the other's home, laughing and playing their guitars. They chuckled at the gossip that spread through town the next morning.

Wayne Buttel and Lillie Loomis saw each other the first time at the general store in Anness, though Lillie was unaware the man who was watching her was Wayne.

Though it was the late 1920s, stepping into the store was like stepping back in time. The building, which sat across the street from the one-room school house, was constructed in the 1800s and had not changed. The slatted wood boardwalk led the way to the wooden door that was framed on either side by huge glass windows. Lined with shelves of various merchandise, the walls of the large single room were barely visible, the exception being the back right corner. There stood a small table and chairs at which local farmers chewed snuff and smoked as they played checkers while comparing notes about farming, catching up on news and spreading local gossip.

Lillie's entrance was announced by the creaky hardwood floor. She felt eyes following her as she headed for a display case on the left that ran the length of the room. The display case held small items of greater value, like jewelry, and the top was crowded with less expensive items. A small clearing, just big enough for a clerk to wait on a customer, was nestled between jars of candy and jars of buttons.

Wayne, sitting among the group of farmers in the back, could not help staring. The rest of the world stopped as Lillie entered the store, bringing in the sun with her golden-blond hair that he later described as the color of ripe wheat.

Taking a break from harvesting, Wayne was filthy and unshaven. His blue eyes gazing at her through his scruffy face made her uncomfortable. She thought he was an old man who should not be looking at a young woman that way. *That old coot!*

A couple of days later, Wayne and Lillie met. Wayne had shaved, and his dark hair was clean and combed. He introduced himself and said he had seen her in the store. "You look a lot like Lyndal Loomis. Are you related?" he asked.

"She's my sister," said Lillie. The two girls were only thirteen months apart and were mistaken for twins more than once.

Lillie had a big part in the Milton High School play in which she sat on a moon and sang as it floated down to the stage. After one of the performances, Wayne approached Lillie and Lyndal as they walked toward their car, asking if the girls would like to go to the local drug store and get malts. Knowing his reputation, Lillie was apprehensive. It took a lot of convincing for the girls to agree, but they did.

A baby's cry jolted Wayne from the past to reality at about 8:00 p.m. on June 28, 1932. When he heard the cry, he thought it was over. But he was wrong. A few minutes later, he heard another cry.

Twins were born–a boy, Charles Arthur, and a girl, Gail Gordine, who was named after Wayne's best friend. Charles was born first, weighing four pounds and five ounces, followed by Gail, weighing one pound and nine ounces. The small country hospital was not equipped to care for premature babies, as it lacked even an incubator.

Lillie was not doing well. There was so much blood in the operating room that a mop was used to clean it up, and tears streamed down Dr. Wallace's face as he told Wayne that he believed none of the three would live. He was so sure the mother and children would die that he recommended the purchase of grave plots.

Wayne's father, William, who was on the board of a small cemetery located about a mile from the farm in Milton where Wayne was born and raised, helped purchase three grave plots. The land included the exact spot where Wayne kissed Lillie for the first time.

A grim shroud covered the small hospital as Wayne and Lillie's families surrounded them with constant prayer. Lillie, who was thirteen in the line of sixteen children, had family at the hospital constantly. A brother, Floyd, came home from California to see her, even though his wife had recently given birth to a baby girl.

Two days after the twins were born, William signed the death certificate of his grandson, Charles.

Wayne didn't know what to do. He was so desperate he headed toward Wichita on foot to get oxygen for his family.

Shortly after that, Gail, who was only as long as a table knife, quit breathing. Dr. Wallace told the nurse to contact the morgue.

"Oh my God, Wayne can't lose all three!" the nurse said to herself. Nurse Sarah Bradley lived on a farm down the road from Wayne's parents and knew the family well. She would not let the baby go without a fight. She went to work on that little girl, trying to resuscitate her.

After working on the tiny body for what seemed like forever, her efforts paid off, and Gail again breathed on her own. The nurse paid special attention to Gail, attending to her every need. She put Gail between hot pads to keep her warm, fed her with an eye dropper and used small pieces of cotton for diapers.

Charles was buried as Lillie and Gail fought for their lives. He was the only one Wayne buried that year.

∞

My mother, Gail Gordine (Buttel) Johnson, was born that June day. Few people of her generation lived through the type of birth she experienced, let alone are able to talk about it.

The biggest miracle is that Mom lived. She lived because

a series of critical decisions were made. If any one of them changed, the outcome would have been very different. Especially the decision made by Nurse Bradley. She did not quit. If she had taken the doctor's order and called the morgue, I would not be here. Her compassion and empathy for my grandfather paved the way for future generations.

My mother came through the birthing experience with cerebral palsy, an injury to the motor area of the brain, although no one knew it right away. It is not hereditary, or caused by the sins of the mother, which was a pervasive thought at the time.

They are not sure if Mom's cerebral palsy happened in those few moments when she was dead or before she was born. Often, one twin takes more oxygen than the other, which could have caused the injury.

The motor area of Mom's brain controlling the right side of her body was most affected, as was her speech. Other parts of her brain had to be trained to take over some of those functions.

To complicate matters, Mom also developed asthma, a disease that constricts the airways in the lungs, making it hard for the body to breath or get enough oxygen.

CHAPTER 2

Diagnosis

The summer Gail was born was one of the hottest Kansas had yet experienced. It was as if her birth ushered in a parching summer breeze. People covered themselves with water-soaked sheets as they slept in an attempt to stay cool, and many people slept outside on their lawns. It was so hot that the wet sheets dried in about thirty minutes.

Recovery after the birth was slow. Lillie and Gail were kept in the hospital for about a month, after which they stayed with a woman in town who took care of them. Doll clothes adorned the baby, and someone made a pair of booties small enough to fit her tiny feet. Mother and child were able to go home on Aug. 8–Lillie and Wayne's first anniversary.

With The Depression in full swing, times were hard. Home for the young family was on the farm with Lillie's parents, Arthur and Effie Loomis. At the time, the Loomis family was very close, both in relationships and proximity. Many of Lillie's siblings and their families farmed in the same area near Anness, which is about forty miles southwest of Wichita.

Dewey and Effie's house was off the road facing the long gravel driveway that continued past the house to the barn and barnyard. The driveway separated the house on the right and a field. A porch, parallel to the driveway, lined the front of the single-level wooden structure.

Across the threshold of the front door was the great room, the biggest in the house, which served as the gathering place for family and friends. The rest of the house was entered through doorways sprinkled around the room. A doorway on the right led to a bedroom, two doorways on the far wall led to a bedroom and a washroom, and a doorway on the left led to the kitchen that ran from the front of the house to the back. There was another room at the back right corner of the house accessible only through the first bedroom.

A long table, lined with benches on either side, filled the center of the kitchen, and was always full of people during meal times. Wherever she lived while growing up, Lillie could not remember a time when only family was at the table during meals. Even with the number of children Arthur, who everyone called by his middle name, Dewey, and Effie had of their own, there was always room for one more child, or farm hand, or friend.

After Gail was born, Dewey and Effie opened their home to Wayne, Lillie and the baby, sharing the space with Lillie's siblings who still lived with their parents. A shoebox placed in an open top drawer of a dresser served as Gail's first crib.

She was so tiny Lillie's size-6 wedding ring slipped over her arm all the way to a shoulder. They were afraid of losing her in a bassinet or crib.

The Loomis genes carry with them a strong intuition, of which Lillie received more than her share. She could sense things before they happened.

Walking into the house the day Wayne brought her and the baby home, Lillie knew something bad was going to happen. She tried to keep Wayne from leaving her side.

"Stay here with me," Lillie begged as Wayne got ready to go out to the field. Somehow, she knew he should not go.

"It's OK. I have work to do. I'll be back later," he said.

"No, you can't go!" Lillie pleaded. "If you go, you're not coming back whole."

Lillie became hysterical and continued begging him to stay with her. Discounting her words, everyone attributed her behavior to the trauma she had been through. The tears changed nothing. Wayne went out to the field anyway.

A couple of hours later, Dewey came in from the field crying. Wayne had been in a farm accident.

"He lost his fingers, didn't he?" Lillie asked.

The first and index fingers of Wayne's left hand had been severed in the gears of a combine, but Lillie did not shed a tear. She had already done her crying.

That hand later became a symbol of strength to Gail. It was the hand she held when Wayne picked her up after she fell, as the anesthetics took over before she went into surgery, and when he was talking with her the night before she got married. It also was the hand she held when she visited him in the nursing home.

Gail was baptized at a Methodist church in Norwich when she was about three months old. As she grew, her family went to many different churches, and Gail was exposed to a variety of theologies.

"You cannot go into a church, any church, with the right attitude and not come out a better person," Wayne always said.

Shortly after Gail was baptized, Wayne found a farm to rent in the vicinity of his two brothers. The three of them had an agreement to help each other, especially during planting and harvest. Their farms were all located about a mile from their parents' home place near Milton.

The home place had been constructed completely by William — the house, the barn, the sheds, everything — and Wayne learned many different trades as he was growing up. He was nine years old when he first plowed an entire field without help from his brothers or father.

Though it appeared like everything would continue as normal, the first few years of Gail's life were far from normal. The physical movements that signify milestones in an infant's life were lacking. She did not play with rattles when she should have. When it came time for her to turn over, sit up or get up on her hands and knees, those things did not happen. Crawling, walking and talking were even farther behind. Her right arm was listless, taking much more energy for it to move, and the hand was not developing the same as the left hand.

Lillie knew something was drastically wrong, but the various doctors to whom she took Gail kept telling her not to worry. Gail was a premature baby and she was just developing slower than normal. They said she would grow out of it.

She didn't.

When Gail was about three years old, Wayne went to renew the lease on the farm and discovered the land had been rented to someone else. The family moved back in with Dewey and Effie.

It was about that time Gail ran away. At three years old, unable to walk, Gail would scoot or stumble around, sometimes using the family dog as a walker. The dog, a mixed breed that looked like a collie, let Gail clasp onto its hair with her left hand and supported her as she slowly stumbled along.

Even then, Gail was served by her strong will and determination. She knew what she wanted and would find ways to move toward that goal.

She wanted to visit her favorite aunt and uncle who lived a few miles down the road. Though her parents said no, she was going to go anyway. Gail stood next to the dog and coaxed it out onto the gravel road.

A couple driving by spotted the tiny child with curly blond hair stumbling down the road alongside the collie. They thought it was odd for her to be out alone, but they knew they could not get near her with the dog as her guardian. The woman walked along with Gail and the dog while the man drove to the nearest farm to see if he could find the child's parents. There he found Wayne and Lillie, who went to get the little vagabonds.

Finding help for Gail continued to be a struggle. Her physical problems had not yet been diagnosed. Her speech was not developing, and her right hand barely functioned.

In trying to help, one of Lillie's sisters suggested Gail be put in an institution for the feeble minded so that everyone could get on with their lives. Hiding handicap family members was not unusual, even when they were kept at home. A broken body also meant a broken mind.

But Gail was blessed with a spunky mother who would not quit. Lillie knew there was more to Gail than her broken body.

"I know the Lord has more for Gail to do than sit in a corner and drool," Lillie would say.

Though Gail could not talk she understood what was said and responded with a type of sign language combined with different sounds. If she wanted water, she would pat her mouth with her left hand and say "Wah wah."

Gail was around four years old when all of that began to change because of Dewey being in the right place at the right time.

*A young Gail. Lillie is hiding in the shrubs
behind Gail holding her up.*

Dewey, like many people, was a creature of habit. That included his visits to the barbershop. Every other Saturday morning, like clock work, he would drive to Wichita to have the same barber at the same barbershop cut his gray hair. One particular Saturday, the barbershop was filled with people, and more were waiting in the street.

Dewey did not have time to wait. He chose a different barbershop a couple of blocks from Wichita State University. It was there, while getting a haircut, that he overheard two men talking about an innovative professor who was starting a program about logopedics–the study and treatment of speech defects. The professor, Dr. Martin Palmer, was establishing the Department of Speech Sciences and wanted his students to work with actual victims, rather than just learn from books and lectures.

The more Dewey listened, the more the symptoms sounded like Gail's, who he had nicknamed Muggy.

When his haircut was finished, he talked with the men, who turned out to be professors at the university. He got Dr. Palmer's phone number, address and more information. He was so excited about the prospect of a program to help Gail.

When Dewey got home, he burst through the door with his sky-blue eyes beaming. "Lillie, I think I finally found the answer for Muggy!" he exclaimed.

Dewey's excitement was infectious, and the family started making phone calls and writing letters. There was an extensive application process for those interested in being part of Dr. Palmer's program. He wanted to make sure the children chosen could benefit from the services his students would provide during their training.

After many interviews and evaluations, which included an extensive family history, Gail was accepted as one of the first 12 students to enter Dr. Palmer's pilot project. It was through this process that she was diagnosed with cerebral palsy. The family finally had a name for Gail's physical limitations and a path to do something about them.

Dr. Palmer was well known because of his work with logopedics. Before accepting the position in Wichita, he was conducting classes for teachers and teaching speech correction methods at Marymount College. He also had a private clinic in Wichita for two years.

He once described speech as "the most complicated function of the brain, a hodgepodge of things that are working on other things–the tongue and jaws, and associated muscles, swallowing, chewing, tasting."

The university hired him in 1934 after it received an endowment to set up a department devoted to speech correction in memory of Ms. Flow Brown.

It took time to accumulate the necessary equipment, set up the laboratory and select the children who would be part of the clinical research. It is not clear when Gail started the application process, but Palmer's first group of children started classes around 1936. Gail went to college when she was four years old, which is something not many people can say.

Dr. Palmer, a caring man with a comedian streak, was given space on the fourth floor of Jardin Hall, the Wichita State University administration building. There he established the Flo Brown Memorial Laboratory. The three-fold program would include clinical services, research and professional training.

There were no elevators in the building, so Gail and the other children were carried up the stairs for classes. Every morning, adults would line the staircase and pass the children up bucket-brigade style, and then take them down the same way when classes were done.

Therapy and treatment at the university included activities that would train other parts of the brain to do what the damaged areas would have done. Not only was Gail going to the university for speech, occupational and physical therapy, her family was working with other doctors to correct some of the physical issues so she could walk.

There was no way the poor farm family could afford the training and surgeries being suggested for Gail, who was born long before insurance became an option. That was where C.Q. Chandler, a banker in Wichita, entered the picture. It is unclear how he found out about Gail, but she reminded him of his own deceased little girl, who also had cerebral palsy. He chose to help Gail and financed a lot of her therapy.

Gail had 13 surgeries on her knees and ankles, all but one by the time she was 8 or 9 years old. During one of those surgeries, the doctors lengthened Gail's heal tendons, tightened the back of her knees and took out her tonsils and adenoids all at the same time. When she came out of surgery, Lillie said they "just butchered her."

Along with financial help, Mr. Chandler often took care of transportation by sending a car to pick up Gail for therapy, which made her feel special. He had a soft spot for children, and Gail was only one of the many he helped. Gail remembers going to his huge home, with a yard that filled a city block, where he would host big parties for children who were in the hospital.

∞

Mom is in the first generation of handicapped people to really be helped. She said she felt a lot of responsibility because of that.

"My mother always told me that I was the first of a minority," said Mom. "Whatever I did would effect the rest of the handicapped coming after."

Mom's strong will and her determination are probably two of the reasons she survived to begin with. Plus she was surrounded by a family that loved her and kept looking for answers.

Dewey being at the right place at the right time, coupled with the family meeting Mr. Chandler, provided the tools necessary to pave the way for Mom to live a normal life. Hope, which is such a small word with such a large meaning, began to blossom.

"Some people would say that my grandfather being in the barbershop that day was a coincidence. But we always said it was an answer to many, many prayers," said Mom.

Mom's religious upbringing was very liberal, which she calls a privilege. The experience of going to many different churches not only helps you understand what others believe, it helps you define what you believe. Through it all, Mom has maintained a strong relationship with God and Jesus Christ. She describes her faith as a "strong faith.... But it's not in any denomination. It is in the Lord."

CHAPTER 3

The Early Years

Living on the farm in Anness, Lillie and Wayne were barely scraping by. Seeking work, Wayne moved the family to Wichita, which also eliminated the commute for Gail's training. He worked at whatever he could find, but jobs were slim pickings, making it hard to pay the rent. The family moved around a lot the next several years.

When Gail was nearly six years old, Dewey died. His death was a moment in time imprinted in Gail's mind.

Through the years, Dewey and Effie had lived several places–Garden Plain, Cheney and Anness, Kansas, and the Pond Creek area of Oklahoma. When Dewey died, they owned the farm near Anness, where they lived during the summers, and a home in Cheney, where they spent the winters. He died out on the farm, and the family had promised not to take him to a funeral parlor. Instead, the morticians came out to the farm and prepared his body for burial in the bedroom, passing everything they needed in and out a window.

The family gathered in the great room of the house as the morticians did their work. Gail said one of the morticians, angry he had to go out to the farm to prepare the body for burial, was not very sensitive to the family. When removing Dewey's blood, he carried it out the front door through the great room.

That night, Effie slept in the same room with Dewey's body. Gail later asked Effie how she could do that.

"Ever since I was 16 I slept in a room with that man. Why would it bother me to sleep in the room with him then?" Effie replied.

The next day the casket was moved to the house in town for the wake, and then buried in the Cheney cemetery.

Gail's training at the university continued. The speech therapy included sucking through a straw, chewing gum and other exercises that improved the reflexes from which speech develops. Communicating with others was getting easier, but people still had a hard time understanding her.

Gail also had physical therapy, which included being suspended above a treadmill in a harness to improve her walking. She said the treadmill, which was made of wood planks on a belt, "sure looked mean."

Just like every other child, Gail also started school in a mainstream classroom when her age dictated.

Because of the family moving around a lot, Gail attended various schools, most of the time scooting and stumbling to and from her classes. The majority of her classes were with able-bodied children, though at Washington Elementary there was a special room called "The Sunshine Room" in which she attended classes with other handicapped children.

Many of Gail's various surgeries were performed during her first few years of elementary school. When she was hospitalized, she continued her classes in a schoolroom at the hospital.

By the time Gail entered school, her left hand functioned normal and was being trained to write, use scissors, etc. Her right hand could grasp things, but was very slow in letting them go. She learned how to use it to help with daily functions, mostly out of necessity.

A new family member was added when Gail was six years old, which elated her. Gail was in the hospital, having been admitted for surgeries on her ankles, when she found out Lillie was pregnant. She wanted a little sister she could play with, and wanted her to be named Ruby after her favorite aunt.

When Lillie visited Gail in the hospital, Gail would pat her tummy and call the baby Ruby.

"Darlene," Lillie would reply.

"No. Ruby," Gail would say.

Gail was home recovering from surgery in October 1938 when the baby was born. Wayne came home from Wesley Hospital to tell Gail that she got her baby sister, but she would not let him say the baby's name. As he tried, she interrupted with, "I know, Darlene."

"Yes, but it is Ruby Darlene," Wayne said.

When Ruby came home, Gail thought she was an adorable child, but she grew to be jealous. Before that, Gail had gotten all the attention, and having a handicap meant a lot of attention was required. Ruby was taking some of that away.

Even though Gail was jealous, she loved the curly-topped, sweet little girl Ruby grew into.

Christmas that year was a tough one for the family. Like most families at the time, money was hard to come by, and the family was struggling to put food on the table let alone celebrate Christmas with all the fixings. Wayne was unhappy with the situation and took matters into his own hands. He wanted Gail to have a Christmas tree, so she was going to have one. On Christmas Eve, the whole family piled into the car and drove just outside of Wichita to a wind break along Highway 54.

"Lillie, watch for the law," Wayne — usually a law-abiding citizen — said as he got out of the car. With Lillie as the lookout, he raced over to the wind break, cut a tree and quickly dragged it back to the car. He secured it on top of the car, and the family sped home before they were caught.

Bringing a tree home on Christmas Eve was not unusual, so none of the neighbors paid any attention. Wayne and Lillie were able to get the tree into the house and set up before anyone noticed.

To decorate the tree, Gail used crayons to color English walnut shells and Lillie cut stars and shapes out of paper. They used thread as hangers to dangle the handmade ornaments on the limbs of the tree. Gail thought it was beautiful. Her eyes beamed the next morning as Lillie said, "Santa told me it was the prettiest tree he had ever seen."

Lillie took Gail's doll, painted the face and made it a new outfit, including booties and a pink bonnet trimmed in lace, and gave it to Gail Christmas morning. Gail knew it was her doll, but it did not matter. She thought it was beautiful.

The next spring, Wayne heard that one could find work about four hours away in Kansas City. He left the rest of the family behind and headed east to see what he could find. That did not last long because an appendicitis visited Wayne, which was complicated by a hernia at the same time. During the surgeries, a screen was installed in his abdomen to keep everything in place.

Being worried about Wayne, Lillie dropped everything to go to his side. She left Ruby with her sister, took Gail and hopped a bus to Kansas City to be with him.

Upon arrival, Lillie went straight to the hospital to see how Wayne was doing. His exhausted body would need a lot of rest to recover.

Being in town only a short time, Wayne had not found an appropriate place for the family to live. He had been staying in a dirt-floor garage, which became the family's first place of residence in Kansas City. Lillie wrote home asking if anyone could help financially. Extra money being a rare commodity, she received only two quarters.

With Wayne unable to work, Lillie had to do something. She found a job at a honky-tonk doing whatever needed to be done.

Music and dancing had always been a part of Wayne and Lillie's lives. Wayne grew up on a dance floor under the watchful eye of his parents, his father performing as the caller at barn and square dances. Blankets would line the dance floor along the walls as substitute beds for when the children got tired. His parents even participated in competitions where they could dance without spilling a drop of water from glasses perched on top of their heads.

As Gail grew up, music and dancing also frequently filled her home. Her parent's friends would show up late in the evening, move aside the rug and furniture, put music on the record player or play the piano, and dance.

It is no surprise that Lillie was hired at the honky-tonk in Kansas City. A hard worker, she mopped floors, took orders, served patrons, danced with patrons, whatever needed to be done. The job included room and board, and Ruby was brought to join the family.

Gail liked living in the rooms in the house connected to the back of the honky-tonk, but she had problems with the owner's daughter, who was about her age. The two girls were together a lot, and the other girl would do naughty things and then tattle on Gail, saying she did them. Being the owner's daughter, Gail was caught between a rock and a hard place. Lillie did nothing about it for fear of losing her job.

When Wayne was well enough to travel, and enough money collected, the family went back to Wichita where Wayne's quest for work continued. Gail resumed working with Dr. Palmer and going to school. She never wore a brace, and her mobility still consisted mainly of scooting and stumbling.

Wayne and Lillie encouraged Gail, never letting her quit. They also would not let her use her handicap as an excuse for not trying.

"There is no shame in not accomplishing something. The shame is in not trying," they would tell her.

Falling was a constant occurrence. When Gail fell, Lillie would pick her up, brush her off, yell at her and send her on her way. The neighbors thought Lillie was terrible, but she kept Gail moving forward, both physically and intellectually.

In 1939, five years after the Flo Brown Memorial Laboratory started, the program received a $10,000 willed donation, and the university allowed it to move to the main level of a different building. They no longer needed to carry the children up four flights of stairs for therapy. The next year, the name of the laboratory was changed to The Institute of Logopedics.

Gail continued working with Dr. Palmer, her time being split between the hospital, school and therapy at the Institute.

She learned to walk the same day Ruby did. She was seven years old and had been in the hospital for an extended period of time, which included another surgery. After the cast had been removed, the doctor picked Gail up out of her chair, turned her head over heals in an air somersault and then set her down on her feet. She hobbled a couple of steps, which was promising.

The doctor sent Gail home from the hospital for a weekend to be with her family but she did not return on Monday. She had come down with the measles. Lillie swore the staff at the hospital knew she was coming down with them and felt that was part of the reason they sent her home. Gail was not allowed back at the hospital until the measles healed, as there were a limited number of beds in the small quarantine wing.

While she was at home, Ruby took a few steps and then began walking. Watching, Gail decided she wanted to do what Ruby had done, so she did. She stood up, squeezing her knees together to catch her balance, hobbled a few steps, and then began to walk. When she got back to the hospital, her walking surprised the doctors.

Soon after Gail got back to the hospital, Ruby got very sick. Gail had inadvertently shared the measles with her sister, which made her so sick she coughed up blood. The "little blonde bundle of joy," as Gail called her, nearly died.

Ruby was at the age where she would get into anything she possibly could, and everything she found had to make it through the mouth test. She would pull things off tables if she could reach them; if she could not reach them, she would pull the table cloth to get to them.

There were no phones in the apartment where they lived, so Lillie had to take or make phone calls from the landlord's apartment. One day, while Lillie was mending something at the kitchen table, she was called away to answer the phone. Ruby pulled on the table cloth and ate straight pins. Lillie did not know what to do. She was afraid of what the pins would do to the little one's insides. She called Sister Georgina, a nurse who worked on Gail's floor at the hospital. Sister Georgina laughed and said, "Give her lots of bread and cake and she will be OK." She said the pins would make it out the other end.

Ruby also had this strange idea that when Gail stood up, it was funny to pull her pants down, after which she would gleefully giggle. Gail did not like it, but Lillie thought it was funny, both because of Gail's reaction and because of Ruby's giggles. Lillie would laugh right alongside Ruby.

A mischievous woman with sparkling eyes, Lillie loved to laugh. She also loved to start controversial conversations, get people going and then sit in the next room and listen. At times, she would stir the pot just to see what would happen.

She also accepted people for whom they are, and cared for others easily. At several of the places they lived, Lillie took in boarders to help with the finances. At one place Wayne and Lillie rented, a large old house with a wooden porch spanning the entire front of the house, Lillie took in five young men looking for work. She cooked for them, did their laundry and ironed their clothes.

The young men, all from the same small town, not only moved into their home, they also moved into their hearts. They became part of the family, which included playing with Gail and Ruby. They often took Gail along when they walked to the soda fountain at the local drug store, making her feel special. Flash, who had beautiful dark hair, taught Gail the confusing skill of telling time. When he would say quarter after, she thought he was talking about the coin, not the minutes.

Though having the boarders made things easier financially, and enlarged the family, it did not help in other ways. Lillie's brother-in-law did not like her, and it gave him an opportunity to spread false rumors about her behavior. He also told Lillie that Gail was the way she was "because of the sins of her mother."

As Gail's surgeries continued, sometimes leaving her in a cast from her waist to her toes, her perseverance grew. She did not quit in her quest for things that she wanted.

Gail was supposed to be immobilized in one of those casts when they lived in the big house. Next door lived a girl about the same age as Gail who would keep her company while Lillie had coffee with the neighbor ladies. One time, the two girls decided they were going to go next door to play and Gail, whose movements were labored and slow, made it all the way down the four or five stairs of the porch to the sidewalk before Lillie caught her. Lillie was surprised that Gail made it that far.

Even with the boarders and financial help from Mr. Chandler, Lillie and Wayne could not keep up with the medical bills. Gail was discharged from the hospital once when she was in a body cast because they could no longer pay the hospital. She was in the cast longer than recommended, and the hospital staff refused to take it off until receiving full payment. A repulsive odor of decay began to radiate from underneath the cast so, Lillie took Gail to the hospital and demanded it be removed. The hospital staff still refused to take it off.

"You take it off now or I will call the sheriff," Lillie replied, which did the trick. The cast came off.

For several years during the late summer and early fall, Lillie and Wayne, along with two other couples, took three combines and followed the harvest north, starting at the tip of Texas and going all the way to the Dakotas. Gail and Ruby would stay with Wayne's parents, William and Ada, at the home place near Milton.

"When those kids came, I thought I would go crazy. When they left, I knew I would," William would say.

The farm was self-sustaining, with dairy cows and beef cattle, chickens, fields of grain and a huge garden filled with vegetables, herbs and flowers. Ada also had every fruit tree that would grow in Kansas in a grove behind the house, and William had honey bees, which he would visit about twice a week to get honey. Ada would plant special flowers just for the bees, though William was not too happy when they spent too much time in the mint. Of course, he would blame Ada.

William also had a grain mill on the farm, and he did the milling for all of the neighbors. He also had a complete blacksmith shop, as well as one of the first cars in the area. In the 1930s, he even had a gas pump on the farm.

Part of a summer day's routine included cooking with stoves in the washhouse, which kept the cooking heat out of the main house. William also had to have his parsley at lunch. Every day Gail and Ruby were sent to pick parsley, and then Ruby would head down the walk to meet William. He once told Wayne that he "would miss that little one with the little curls coming to meet him at noon."

In the evenings, children from down the road would come over and they all would play hide-and-seek and Annie-Annie-Over.

At other times during the summers, Wayne and Lillie would pack up the girls and head out to Annes to help Lillie's brothers in their fields. It was during one of those excursions that Gail nearly hung herself.

The women had been cooking and decided they were not taking the lunch out to the field. They sent Gail to tell the men that lunch was ready, but they would have to come up to the house to get it. On her way out, at the edge of the field, Gail fell, like she always did, but this time she landed on strands of barbed wire that caught her right under her chin. The men saw her fall and came running immediately. She was lucky to only receive a scar.

Mom has said, "When one person in a family is handicapped, the whole family is." She was blessed with a family that looked out for her, and tried to protect her while helping her to strive for independence. They did not coddle her, or allow her to use her handicap as an excuse to quit. They did not treat her like a victim, nor would they give her sympathy if she behaved like one. She was like everyone else; she just had to work a little harder.

Through many physical therapy sessions, Mom's walking got better and better, but she always walks with a limp. Her gait is slower, and her center of balance is much different than most people. Mom's speech has gotten clearer with time, but it has always had a slur, especially when she is tired.

Even with her family often struggling to survive, Mom's home was filled with love, friends and music. When I was growing up, Grandma and Grandpa would still dance in their living room. The carpet did not deter Grandpa from leading anyone across the floor, even me.

CHAPTER 4

Growing up

While Lillie took care of her family and boarders, Wayne took whatever job he could get. They were able to keep the big house until Japan hit Pearl Harbor in 1941, which put the United States right in the thick of the war. Four of the boarders joined the Army, and Wayne landed a job at Beech Aircraft working as a mechanic.

Gail was nine years old when Lillie and Wayne bought a house for the first time; a small two-bedroom, single-level home on the corner of Minneapolis and 22nd streets in Wichita. It also had a bathroom, living room, kitchen, laundry room and a single-stall garage, and Lillie boasted that it was the only one in the neighborhood that had space for a table in the kitchen. The home was part of a new housing complex constructed for war airplane factories. Between 1941 and 1945, the factories employed more than 25,000 people in Kansas, most of those in the factories in Wichita.

The house was purchased when Gail was in the hospital, and kept a surprise until she was brought home. With the purchase came a feeling of security for Gail, erasing the constant worry of having to move again.

Lillie made sure she turned the little house into a home. She added a flagstone walk that went from the concrete front porch to the sidewalk, took care of the yard, and planted flowers and vegetables. The last boarder in the big house also came to live with them, and he slept on a roll-away bed in the living room.

Three times a week, Gail was going to therapy at the Institute of Logopedics, which incorporated in 1945. It was after one of her therapy sessions, shortly after moving to the new house, that she met Joy, who became a life-long friend.

Born in Topeka, Kansas, Joy had lived in Twin Falls, Idaho, before moving to Wichita. Her parents, Mildred and Marshal Craft, bought a small yellow house on 22ⁿᵈ Street, around the corner from Gail's house. Marshal was hired at one of the airplane factories and Mildred, a teacher before moving to Wichita, got a part-time job at Safeway. Both Joy and Gail were the new kids on the block.

On the drive home, Wayne asked Gail how the therapy session went; and then chatted about the schedule for the rest of the day. As they were getting out of the car in the driveway, Joy, a small, dark-haired, purple-freckled girl, walked up and introduced herself to Gail. The purple freckles came from medication dotting her face to treat impetigo. Joy had seen Gail come and go for several days, and thought it would be interesting to find out more about her. They started talking and a friendship blossomed.

Though Gail's speech was slurred, Joy was quickly able to understand most of what she said, and was not afraid to ask questions to understand better. They found out they were about the same age, had a lot in common and enjoyed many of the same things. They spent much of the remainder of the summer together.

Gail said Joy "was an extra wise and compassionate little girl."

The next fall, Gail and Joy started fourth grade together in a small four-room elementary school, but Gail put herself back into third grade. Having spent so much time in the hospital the previous school year, she was afraid she missed something. Her parents, in their infinite wisdom, let her decide which grade to attend.

Even though Joy was one grade ahead, they still had some classes together. In one, the teacher asked students who they thought had the best vocabulary. Joy raised her hand. When called on, she named Gail, which surprised everyone. When the teacher asked why, Joy responded, "Because, when she can't say a word, she has to tell me what it means."

The two girls continued to spend a lot of time together, in and out of school. Knowing Gail could never move fast enough to get a swing during recess, Joy would run out to the playground to save one for her. The only problem was that Gail got so she would expect to spend all of recess with Joy every day, which was frustrating for Joy, who also wanted to play with others. Joy's mother suggested she arrange time to play with Gail and also time to play with others, which worked well for both of them.

Because they were together so much, Joy got to the point where she understood Gail's speech much better than others. She ended up playing the role of interpreter. When people could not understand Gail, the would ask Joy what she said.

World War II was in full force, and everyone in the United States was involved. Everything was saved, down to the bacon grease. Ration stamps were handed out for items like sugar, flour and shoes, so those things could be sent over to the troops. Because Gail walked more on her toes than on the soles of her feet, she quickly went through shoes. Other family members would save their shoe stamps for her.

Lillie worked with the Red Cross, and also was an air raid warden in charge of a specific area. During a blackout, it was her job to make sure her area was completely dark. Her duties included directing a group of people to wander through the area checking for light leaking out of homes, perhaps through cracks in curtains, or for outside lights that were not extinguished. Even radios had to be covered because light from the dial might be seen from the air.

Elementary students also got involved, collecting paper at the school for the war drive. If a student behaved well, did her work quickly, and was trustworthy, a trip down to the collection room to separate and bundle the paper for recycling was in order. Joy and Gail frequently made that trip together.

The girls would often cheat and browse through the magazines they were bundling, sometimes tearing out photographs or stories they wanted to keep. One time, Gail saw a full-page photograph of a horse in a Red Horse gasoline ad, which she wanted. Joy also wanted it, and Gail knew Joy had a tender heart. She also knew Joy did not like to see anything destroyed.

"If I can't have it, I'll tear it up," said Gail as she sat poised to tear the photograph in half. Joy let her have it.

When caravans of soldiers would drive through town, students would race out of the school and stand at the corner on 21st Street to watch, waving as the soldiers went past. The soldiers were kind enough to wave back.

Next door to Joy lived a boy named Bob, who had a little red half-terrier and half-chow puppy that looked like a little teddy bear. His mother said he could not keep the puppy and had to find it a different home. He decided he would give it to Gail, thinking that once Lillie and Wayne saw her with the puppy they would let her keep it. After Gail had an asthma attack, he came over with a bowl of peaches in one hand and the puppy in the other. He was right. Lillie and Wayne could not refuse the puppy, which Gail named Dolly.

Dolly later had nine puppies, though Gail's family did not realize there were that many. She chose to have the puppies under the plants in the front yard when the family was at a baseball game. When they got home, Lillie and Wayne heard whining coming from under the plants. Wayne got down on his hands and knees searching for the source of the whine. He found a puppy, brought it in the house and headed back out to get more. Lillie prepared a bed for the puppies as Wayne brought in another puppy, and then another, and another, and another.

"Wayne, is there any end to it?" Lillie asked.

By the time Wayne was finished, there were nine puppies snuggled together with their mother in their new bed.

When the puppies were weaned, homes needed to be found. Gail wanted to give the puppies away but Wayne refused. He said people take better care of animals when they pay for them. If they get them free, they treat them as expendable. If they pay something for them, even if it is only one dollar, they take better care of them. He made nine dollars selling those puppies.

When Gail was twelve years old, she decided she wanted to learn to ride a bicycle, and asked her parents to get her one. With all the surgeries and therapy she had gone through, Lillie and Wayne did not know how to answer her. They did not want to undo any of what had been done, so they took her to the doctor to discuss it with him.

"Don't let her try to ride a bike because she will not be able to, and it will damage her self esteem," he said. He never mentioned any concerns of destroying progress that had been made by the surgeries.

"You heard what the doctor said. What do you want to do?" Gail was later asked by her parents.

"I want to learn to ride a bike," Gail replied. So Wayne went out and bought her a bicycle. Once she started working on it, she did not quit. It took about six months to learn to ride the bicycle on her own, with Joy running next to her for hours, days and months to help her.

Stopping without falling was the hardest part. "We had to catch her when she stopped," said Joy. If not, Gail ended up with bloody knees.

Many Saturdays were spent on that mission.

Saturday nights were movie nights in the neighborhood. The children would gather in a group and walk the mile to the NoMar Theater, on the corner of 21st and Waco streets, where they could see the movies on the silver screen for ten cents admission. That was one of Gail's favorite activities.

Wayne thought the distance to the theater was too far for Gail to walk because of the uneven terrain and railroad tracks they needed to cross. He would drive her there to join her friends.

In 1945, as the war ended, the airplane factories in Kansas had mass lay offs, with one factory in Wichita laying off 16,000 workers in one day. Wayne was cut from Beechcraft.

They sold their house, and Lillie and the girls moved to an upstairs apartment in Pratt, Kansas, where Lillie opened a beauty shop with six chairs. Wayne, who found a job at a large machine shop in Wichita, moved into his employer's home.

The small commercial space that housed the beauty shop on street level had a large glass window through which could be seen all six chairs. Lillie had several other beauticians working with her, and they charged one dollar for a wash and set.

Having more than one chair was a new concept in beauty shops, and people in Pratt did not readily accept the idea. The business did not last long. Lillie ended up closing the doors while she still had a little bit of money, and put that toward renting a one-chair beauty shop on Douglas Street in Wichita. She bought the equipment, owned by Lyndal's sister-in-law, on installments.

Lillie and the girls moved in with Wayne at his employer's home, where they stayed until they raised enough money to purchase a home. They bought a five-bedroom house on Holyoke Street, and rented three of the bedrooms to veterans. Lillie closed the shop on Douglas Street and moved her equipment into a large room off the kitchen that she converted into a beauty shop. She hired a beautician, who worked at the shop every day.

The city did not take kindly to the beauty shop being operated in a home separate from the beautician's residence. Businesses in residential areas were only to be conducted by those living in the building. To get around the law, they hung some of the beauty operator's clothing in the closet.

The beauty shop operated until the equipment was repossessed. Instead of giving Lillie time to pay it off, Lyndal's husband, Marvin, talked his sister into taking back the equipment.

By this time, Ruby was growing into a beautiful young girl who looked older than her years. People were drawn to her blonde hair, green eyes and ready smile. Gail and Ruby got along OK, but there were times when jealousy still reared its ugly head–Gail jealous of the attention Ruby drew, and Ruby envious of all the attention Gail needed.

Ruby never liked her name, and in the fourth or fifth grade, she asked if she could be called by her middle name instead. From then on, she was called Darlene.

Gail's therapy at the Institute had pretty much ended.

The doctors were recommending one more surgery to lengthen the tendons in her ankles, though they did not know if it would do any good. The goal was to help her walk flatter on the soles of her feet, while at the same time making it easier to not drag her toes. The chances of it making a difference were about 50 percent.

"You heard what the doctor said. Now what do you want to do?" Lillie and Wayne asked Gail.

They talked about it for a while, discussing the pros and cons of having the surgery, after which Gail replied, "I think I'll have it done." Gail later asked Wayne what he would have done if she had decided to not have the surgery. He said the decision was hers, so the surgery would not have happened.

Gail, at thirteen years old, made the right decision. Her last surgery did help, and she was able to walk for many more years than the doctors expected.

After the surgery healed, and Gail was nearly fifteen years old, she decided she wanted to take ballroom dance classes. Ballroom dancing was big at the time, and most young people took classes. In checking around, her parents found Wichita School of Fine Arts, a well known dance studio owned by Eileen Rhodes that had its beginning as part of the University of Wichita. The studio taught just about any type of dance, and the school also had drama classes.

Lillie took Gail to see the studio, meet Eileen and inquire about classes. They ended up enrolling Gail in one that met on a weekly basis. She really enjoyed the classes and was not shy, which impressed the instructors. When it was time for girls to choose their partners, she was right up there asking a boy to dance.

Wayne was able to pay for one block of classes, but no more. Wanting to continue, Gail talked to Eileen explaining the family's situation and that she was going to have to quit. She asked if there was anything she could do in trade for the cost of continued classes.

"We'll work something out," said Eileen. A snack bar was due to open, and Eileen offered Gail a job working behind the counter. She worked in the snack bar Friday nights and Saturdays to pay for her instruction, and later became Eileen's "girl Friday." Gail continued taking ballroom dance classes, and later added drama classes. She also tried tap dance, but she could not get her feet and legs to work fast enough.

Gail with her cousin, Dixie, and her father, Wayne.

When Gail entered Wichita High School East, a three-story brick building completed in 1923, she was given the option to use the freight elevator instead of the stairs to get from floor to floor. She chose not to, and even though she hobbled up and down the stairs between classes, she arrived on time.

She was in mainstream classes, including the required physical education class. Her physical limitations were not accommodated, so Gail spent the period playing Chinese checkers.

"It was a waste of time," said Gail. She felt she should have had the option to take a different class and learn something, but the school administration's hands were tied. Gail had to attend physical education, though she did not participate in the activities.

At sixteen years old, Gail missed another year of school because she was anemic, spending the entire year at home in bed. She ended up with a kitten from Joy, whose pregnant cat had been hit by a car. In order to save the kittens, they had to be surgically removed. Gail received a kitten to keep her company, which she named Ginger.

The first time Gail left the house, Ginger got very upset. She searched through the whole house looking for her, even jumping up on the chest of drawers and cupboards.

Ginger was possessive of Gail and the family home. When she had a litter of kittens, one of them became part of the family, much to the chagrin of Ginger. She responded by going to the family across the alley, but would come home once in a while to see if the kitten was still there. She would walk through the house, and if she saw the kitten, she went back to the other family.

"If she wants to act like that, she can stay there," said Wayne.

One exception the high school granted Gail was the ability to take its Family Living class when she was a junior. It was a class reserved for the seniors, but Gail wanted to take it early.

In the class, girls were paired with a boy who would be their husband for the duration of the class. They would shop for groceries, search for an apartment and research what it would cost for utilities, transportation, etc. Infants were brought in, and the couples fed them and changed diapers. The goal was to educate the students on the expenses and responsibilities of living on their own and of having a family.

Though Gail was older than the majority of seniors, the school initially refused to let her in the class. Wayne and Lillie finally talked the administration into changing its mind.

While in high school, Gail spent her summers with family in Cheney, often staying with Lyndal and Marvin and their five children. She also would babysit another uncle's four children.

Dixie, the oldest of Lyndal and Marvin's children, belonged to a Wednesday night church youth group and Gail tagged along.

The summer she was seventeen years old, the youth group was raising money for a trip to the pastor's three mountain cabins in Colorado. Gail worked alongside the members at bake sales and car washes, doing whatever she could to help raise money.

When it came time for the money to be distributed, the pastor said he felt one more member should go. "Gail has worked right alongside us. I think she should be included," he said.

Everyone agreed, and the money raised was enough to pay all but ten dollars of each member's trip. Gail did not have the ten dollars, so Ron, a boy she was dating at the time, said he would pay. Lyndal would not allow it. She said Gail "would not be beholden to anyone." Lyndal and her sister, Ruby, both chipped in five dollars so Gail could go.

The week-long trip included a hike up Mount Chautauqua, and Gail went along. The hike was not easy, but she did not quit. With the help of others in the group, she made the climb.

"If you would have told me Gail would climb a mountain, even with the help from the guys, I would not have believed it!" the pastor said afterwards.

Gail on a mountain with youth group friends.

When the summer ended, life for Gail in Wichita went back to normal. Along with going to school and working at the dance studio, Gail and her mother both took jobs at the all-night drug store across Hillside Avenue from Wesley Hospital. Things went well for Lillie, but not for Gail. She was fired because she was slow to catch on to some of the pricing. Items were not priced individually, and Gail had to check the shelves for prices when people came to the counter to pay.

"I was so up tight about doing it right that I made it harder than it needed to be," said Gail. "I was too slow. I was trying to impress the owner and it didn't work."

That was about the same time "Speech Town" was born, with the help of an FHA loan. The Institute of Logopedics moved into its new red brick buildings constructed on a forty-four-acre piece of property on 21st Street. The campus had a long horseshoe driveway with a large administration and school building at the end. Along both sides of the horseshoe were single-level fourplexes that housed families of the residential students. The Institute also had 24 field laboratories throughout Kansas.

Though therapy had ended a few years earlier, Gail was still in contact with teachers, staff and others she had met at the Institute, and was an advocate for handicapped people. Her public speaking career began in 1950 when she traveled all over the state of Kansas doing presentations to raise funds for the Institute.

"It was my way of giving back," she said.

Virgil Barret, a speech and physical therapist from the Institute, traveled with Gail, both as a representative from the Institute and as her chaperone. When Gail stepped up to the microphone with her blonde hair, wearing the pink floral print dress she and Joy had made, Virgil said she looked like an angel.

While in High school, Gail also joined Handicap Plus, a club that paired handicapped people with able-bodied people, called "Good Sports," who helped them with whatever they needed at the meetings.

Gail's Aunt Helen discovered the club while she was working as a telemarketer selling magazines. One of her prospective customers was a member and through their conversation, explained how it worked. Helen got excited because she thought it would be something Gail would enjoy.

She was right. Gail did enjoy the meetings. The club also gave presentations, in which she participated.

As a little girl, Gail fell in love with movies and had hoped to one day be an actress. She went to as many movies as possible, and collected movie memorabilia. Along with giving back to those who helped her, public speaking gave her the opportunity to perform.

∞

Children and teenagers can sometimes be cruel to those who are different. Mom said she does not remember being treated badly in school because of her handicap, though Joy begs to differ. Joy said there were those who were mean to Mom, and that Mom is so forgiving she has forgotten.

"I was such a brat," said Mom. "Joy was very patient with me."

Mom remembers being asked a lot of questions about why she is the way she is, and she loved educating people about cerebral palsy, but she does not remember being abused in any way. Though she was the last one to be chosen for games, she said she was not excluded.

"I had my group of friends, and the funny part is they were the most intelligent students, and the wealthiest," said Mom. "It just did not fit what you hear about being an outcast."

When Mom did her public speaking, she not only told people about the Institute, she told them about life for handicapped people. "They are the same as anyone else," she said. "You don't throw away a present because the package is broken."

That was just the beginning of her being an advocate for handicapped people, and she has not quit. She continues to make a difference by speaking up.

CHAPTER 5

---- ✦ ----

Beyond High School

A girl Gail barely knew approached her near the end of her senior year of high school explaining she had watched her go up and down the stairs every day, which inspired her to keep going. If Gail could do it, so could she.

"I would not have finished high school if not for you. Thank you," she said.

The year 1953 was a big year for Gail. She graduated from East High School, headed to college and was involved in the first of numerous telethons for the Institute of Logopedics.

At one local telethon, Gail made the mistake of saying "thank you to all who supported," which organizers said spoiled the impact of the cute little girl saying "thank you" with the song "You'll Never Walk Alone" playing in the background. Gail, who felt you could never say "thank you" enough, said as punishment, she was not allowed to appear on "This is Your Life" for Dr. Palmer.

At another telethon, Gail made earrings out of artificial flowers to be auctioned off by Amanda Blake, the actress who played Kitty on the television series Gunsmoke. Amanda was able to get $100 for a pair.

After graduation, Gail chose to go to Friends University, a three-building Quaker college located in Wichita. She could have gone to the state university, which would have been less expensive, but she felt it was too big. Gail did not want to become "just a number." She also wanted the life experience of living away from home in a dormitory.

Gail's parents were thrilled with her decision, but coming up with the tuition was a struggle. Somehow they made it happen, and in the fall of 1953, Gail moved into the large white house across the street from the college that served as the girl's dormitory. She shared a room on the top floor of the three-level building.

There were three rooms and a bathroom on her floor; one room at the top of the stairs with three beds in it, which is where Gail stayed, and two other rooms that each had two beds.

Joanne Blaire, a friend who graduated from high school one year before Gail, also lived on the same floor in one of the smaller rooms, sharing it with a girl named Phyllis. The college was pretty flexible with the girl's living quarters, allowing them to remodel and paint the rooms to fit their individual personalities. Joanne's father had added bookshelves to their room, and Phyllis painted the walls yellow.

Not having any specific plans for painting her room, Gail found a bucket of yellow liquid she thought was paint and a paint roller. She rolled the liquid onto the walls. The first coat seemed a bit thin, so she put on another, and the walls dried a pale shade of yellow. When Phyllis got home, she was furious. The liquid was not paint; it was the water Phyllis had used to rinse out the roller.

"How could you be so stupid?" she asked Gail. And so it went. Phyllis never warmed up to Gail, and searched for reasons to be rude to her.

To attend classes, the girls walked across the street and up the half-block sidewalk to the stately university building, constructed in 1887. Light posts lined the sidewalk from the street to the front stairs, where several other sidewalks spread like spider legs to other parts of the block. The vast lawn, dotted with trees and park benches, was one of Gail's favorite places on campus.

"On a cold, crisp winter evening, when the snow glistened, and the chimes rang, there was nothing like it," Gail said.

At the top of about twenty concrete stairs, pillars surrounded by concrete supported a large stone archway sheltering the main building's front door. Entering the door put the students in a large foyer with an office in about fifty feet. Wide hallways with hardwood floors opened up on both sides leading to grand wood staircases ascending to the second level, where classrooms with high ceilings and wooden floors were located.

The other two buildings on the campus housed the cafeteria and commons, and the gymnasium. There also was a small stadium and football field.

Gail took all the normal freshman classes, except math, which she planned to take the next year. She also took art classes. Her goal was to be either an interior decorator or a librarian, which led her to work in the college library creating monthly posters for the main bulletin board. Not realizing the college had a professor with the last name Casper, her first project was a poster on which Casper the Friendly Ghost was cutting up a book saying, "I can't put down a book until I finish it." When the librarians saw it, they laughed and told Gail about the professor.

The young Professor Casper got a big kick out of the poster, even though it provided fodder for others to tease him. "I thought you knew how to read," people would say. Gail was paid extra for the project, so she was pleased with the professor's response.

Besides working in the library, Gail had a job as a bookkeeper for an insurance agent she met through a handicap club. One of her required courses in high school was bookkeeping, which Gail barely passed. She had an awful time because all the problems were written out, which is much different from a bill in hand. When working with a bill, there is no question if it is a debit or a credit. The teacher passed Gail with a D because she did not want to have have her in the class again. A D was more than she deserved.

"I always laughed about that, doing bookkeeping for a living after nearly failing it in high school," said Gail.

College also was a time of exploration into the Quaker way of life. About a block from the dormitory was the Friend's University Church, which is where Gail learned the Quaker way of worship. The students received a one-half credit for going to chapel every morning.

It also was a time of "coming out" socially. Gail began dating more and spending more time at social events. She had few dates in high school; mostly blind dates arranged by Joy. "I wanted her to have something to do," said Joy.

Gail's first date was with a tall young man with red hair and freckles named Rex Niece. The couple went to Joyland, an amusement park on Central Avenue in Wichita, with Joy and Johnny Belt.

By the time Gail was in college, Joy and Rex were married. The couple had moved to Colorado where Rex was stationed after he joined the Army.

Gail with her sorority sisters.

In college, Gail joined the Alpha Gama Alpha Neu sorority, volunteering time at various organizations alongside her sorority sisters, one of which was the USO. McConnell Air Force Base is located near Wichita, and the USO provided a place for the airmen to relax and enjoy female company. It was there, on a Sunday afternoon, that she met her future husband.

On July 3, 1954, during the Korean Conflict, Air Force PFC Arnold J. Johnson was at the USO playing cards as Gail played ping pong with another airman, Joe Ferrue. She noticed the tall, thin man with dark hair and dark eyes playing cards, but thought he must be a terrible bore. Instead of talking with one of the younger women, he chose to play cards with the senior hostess.

Arnold also noticed Gail, who was barely five feet tall with blonde hair and eyes that changed from blue to green, reflecting the color of the clothes she wore. He motioned Joe over to him, said he wanted to meet Gail, and asked Joe if he thought she would let him take her home.

"Ask her. All she can do is say no," said Joe, who later made the introductions. Gail and Arnold chatted for a polite minute, and then Gail continued to play ping pong with Joe.

When the USO closed, Gail headed out the door of the large old building and across the concrete front porch to the long flight of stairs leading to the street.

"Hey you! Wait up!" Gail heard from behind. Arnold was running after her. She paused on the stairs and waited for him to catch up. He asked if he could take her home.

"No. You know the rules," Gail replied. She reiterated the rule that forbade the volunteers to date the airmen. She had fifteen cents in her pocket for the bus fare.

As they walked down the stairs, he tried to convince her to let him take her home, and when he asked again, she said "no."

Standing at the bottom of the stairs, they talked for a few minutes, and then he asked again. She said "no" and headed toward the bus stop. He put a hand on each shoulder and turned her the opposite direction. Needless to say, he ended up taking her home in his black 1940 Ford rag-top convertible, a car he had purchased with several other airmen. By the time he met Gail, he had bought out the other men's shares and was the sole owner of the car.

When they drove away from the USO, he asked if he could buy her dinner. They landed at the Cow Cow drive-in restaurant, which served things like hamburgers and malts.

Leaving the restaurant, Arnold purposefully made a wrong turn so he would not have to immediately take her home.

"You do that again, and I will start screaming," Gail said.

"You know, I think you would," he replied.

He drove her straight to her home on North Falustia Street, where they sat in front of the house talking. Sitting in the front yard, still as a statue, was Whacky, the family's pet duck.

Whacky joined the family as a fuzzy little yellow duckling on a bright Easter morning. A gift to Darlene, Whacky grew up playing with Puddles, the family's dog. The two of them became good friends, and would curl up together to sleep. When Whacky was full grown, he was banished to the yard. If Puddles was in the house too long, Whacky would call for him to join him in the yard.

Whacky also took on the role of Gail's nanny, though she was an adult. Whacky would follow Gail the two blocks to the bus stop, flapping his wings and quacking, which was embarrassing. People who rode the bus enjoyed the spectacle. As the bus approached the stop, they would lean forward in anticipation of seeing Gail and the duck. When Gail got on the bus, Whacky would turn around and go home, sometimes returning to greet her when she later got off the bus.

Arnold thought the duck was a lawn ornament and jumped when Whacky moved, sending Gail into fits of giggles.

By the time Arnold said good-night, the two had a date to see a movie the next evening, which was Wayne's birthday. Their first date was seeing the movie "The Ten Commandments." Arnold had planned to see a western film, but Gail was more interested in the other one.

Arnold, who was about six-feet-four-inches tall, with dark hair and brown eyes, had never been around handicap people enough to be comfortable. In fact, he later told Gail he could not stand to be around them. Though Gail limped and her right hand was visibly handicapped, Arnold did not notice, even as she hobbled down the long staircase in front of the USO. All he had seen was her blonde hair and blue eyes. Later, he told her he did not realize she was different until the third date, which was too late. By then, he was already in love with her.

"God blinded me just long enough that it didn't matter any more," Arnold said.

One week after they met, Arnold asked Gail to go steady, to which she promptly told him "no." She said she would have to think about it. Three days later, Gail called Arnold at work and asked if the offer was still good.

"Why didn't you wait until I was with you to tell me?" Arnold said.

The relationship grew as they spent a lot of time together. Arnold was at the house so often he practically lived there. They learned a lot about each other – he did not like pets in the house, they belonged outside; she loved any kind of pet, especially cats and dogs; he played a variety of instruments and had a band when he was in high school; she grew up with music and dancing filling her home; he loved taking photographs and developing them in a darkroom; she liked turning spaces into beautiful places; family was important to both of them, and they both wanted to raise children.

On Aug. 10, six weeks after they met, Arnold proposed to Gail. He had called Lillie ahead of time telling her he had something special planned. He asked her to make sure Gail wore jeans for their date that evening.

When Arnold picked Gail up, they drove around aimlessly for a while.

"What are we going to do?" said Gail.

"Oh, nothing much," Arnold replied. "Let's go to the park and just sit, or walk around."

He pointed the car in the direction of Riverside Park, an extensive park along the riverbanks of the Arkansas River where it winds through Wichita. Though he made it seem spontaneous, Arnold had put a lot of thought into the evening.

"Oh, I forgot to tell you, I have a picnic lunch," said Arnold as he opened the door to let Gail out of the car. He went to the trunk and pulled out a blue wool Air Force blanket and a basket of food. He set up the picnic near the river, across from the lighted boathouse. As the evening grew darker, the lights reflected off the river, adding a romantic ambience.

After they had eaten, Arnold said, "How would you like to be an airman's wife?"

"That would depend on who the airman was," replied Gail, mischief dancing in her eyes.

"Darn it Gail! I'm asking you to marry me."

They were married about four months later. When Arnold first saw Gail, he decided he wanted to marry her. Gail did not believe in love at first sight, but he made a believer out of her. She liked Arnold. He was nice, and he also was good looking, but Gail believes she fell in love with him because he loved her so much.

Gail was mischievous, and said she was lucky he still wanted her after she made it so difficult for him to propose. "With you, life will never be boring," Arnold told her.

When Gail told Darlene she was going to marry Arnold, she responded, "Of all the guys you dated, you're going to marry him?! You're kidding, right?" Darlene did not like him because she thought he was arrogant.

"No," responded Gail.

"You're not kidding," said Darlene, and she took a deep breath.

Darlene was already planning her own wedding, which was set for the middle of October. Though she was only sixteen years old, she had grown into a lovely young woman. Her body had developed the curves of a woman at a young age. When she was twelve years old, ticket sellers at movie theaters would not believe she was younger than Gail. To prevent the long arguments that would ensue, they chose to purchase a child ticket for Gail and an adult ticket for Darlene.

With blonde hair, green eyes and the curves of someone older, Darlene caught the eye of Ernie Spriggs, who was nineteen years old at. When Darlene asked permission to marry Ernie, Wayne and Lillie knew she was strong willed; that they would probably lose her if they said no. They gave their permission on the condition that she would finish high school, which she never did.

On Aug. 15, Gail was a bridesmaid in a wedding, where she wore a calf-length, pale turquoise organdy dress with a knot in the back. Arnold told her it would make a perfect wedding dress. Gail's Aunt Helen took fabric from the knot at the back and made a veil to match the dress.

The engagement ring soon followed. It was payday, and Arnold showed up at the house when Gail and Darlene were still in bed in the room they shared. Lillie and her sister-in-law, Pauline, were sitting at the table in the kitchen having coffee when Arnold knocked on the door. As she opened the door, Lillie could see the bulge in his pocket.

"Can I go into the bedroom and talk with Gail?" he asked.

"Just a minute," said Lillie. She peeked in to make sure the girls were decent before letting him in the room.

"I got something for you," he said to Gail as he kneeled on the floor beside the bed, pulling out the ring.

Gail looked at the ring as he put it on her finger, which is when Darlene woke up. "Arnie Johnson, what are you doing in my bedroom?" Darlene cried.

"Giving me this," said Gail as she showed her the ring.

"This isn't the place to do that!" said Darlene.

All the while, Lillie and Pauline were sitting in the kitchen whispering, giggling and getting a kick out of the whole situation. At the time, it was pretty risque for a man to be in a woman's bedroom unless they were married, no matter what the circumstances.

"What are you going to tell your children about how you got your ring?" Lillie later asked Gail.

Getting engaged was the easy part. The next phase was where the work began. Arnold grew up in the Catholic church, even serving as an alter boy. At the time they got engaged Gail was going to a Methodist church. In the 1950s, theirs would be called a mixed marriage.

Arnold had to get permission to get married from his Air Force commander, which was no problem; and because he was only nineteen years old, he also had to get permission from his parents, which was a challenge.

When he first called his mother, Ethel, she said, "no". She used the excuse he was too young and should wait until he was twenty years old. She also said things like, "You don't love her, you love the family. You really like her father." She told Arnold that Wayne saw Arnold coming as a chance for someone to take Gail off his hands.

She also said, "Why buy the cow when you can get the milk for free?"

Ethel was pregnant with Arnold when she married Ragner, though Arnold did not realize it until after he and Gail were married. Ragner's mother, Lena, never liked Ethel and said mean things about her, which could have been part of the reason Ethel said mean things about Gail.

Arnold assured her that his relationship with Gail was not like that, and eventually told her, "Either you sign the papers or we will go someplace, like Tennessee, where we can get married without your permission."

Ethel finally relented and signed the papers, though she never thought Gail was good enough for Arnold.

Once across that hurdle, the priest challenged their decision to marry. "Of all the nice Catholic girls, why did you choose a protestant?" he asked Arnold. The priest and Arnold went round and round, with Arnold fighting for the right to marry Gail.

Then the Catholic instruction for Gail began, and at its completion, she had to give up everything in her own faith. The papers she was supposed to sign stated she would baptize and raise the children Catholic, name them after saints and not talk to them about her own faith. The inability to name the children whatever she wanted and share her faith with them were the last straws.

"I'll name my child Fido if I want to," Gail snapped at the priest while Arnold, standing behind the priest, shook his head trying to get her to calm down.

"I think we should end this for today," said Arnold.

As they were driving away, Gail gave him back the engagement ring. She said she was ready to throw in the towel. He pulled over and they sat by the side of the road talking about it for quite a long time.

"You would be the one who would be with the children the most, and there is no reason you couldn't say whatever you wanted to them," he told her.

She still refused the sign the papers, feeling she could not sign something she knew she would not follow.

"I'll take the ring back for now, but let's pray about it for three days and then decide," said Arnold.

On the evening of the third day, he took her to dinner at a local grill. "I will marry you any time, any place," he said. "But if I did, it would hurt so many people." It was important to his family that they were married by a Catholic priest.

"I know how you feel. You know how I feel," Arnold continued. "Most importantly, God knows how we feel." He told her to go ahead and sign the papers, even though they both knew they would not follow through with everything written on them.

Gail did sign the papers, and the wedding was back on, though the priest still continued to do everything in his power to stop it. He kept putting it off because he said he forgot to tell them something. He continually tried to discourage them from getting married.

The date was finally set for October 24, one week after Darlene and Ernie's wedding. Ethel wanted to be at her first-born's wedding, though Ragner said the family could not afford to take the trip from Escanaba, Michigan to Wichita. Taking the train was free because Ragner worked at the docks on Lake Michigan for the Chicago NorthWestern Railroad, but the time away from work and the other expenses were more than he felt they could spend. Ethel decided she was going to go anyway, and sneaked out to the train station where she hopped a train to Wichita before Ragner even knew she was gone. Then the priest put the wedding off again, which meant Ethel could not be there. She only had a couple of days before she had to get back to Escanaba.

Through the planning, work continued for both–Arnold at the airport and Gail at the dance studio. A close bond had developed between Gail and Eileen, and Eileen wanted to help with the wedding. She gave Gail part of her trousseau, taking her shopping and buying her a negligee and two dresses. They had to go to multiple stores because Gail was so small and most stores did not carry dress sizes smaller than a nine.

The night before the wedding, Wayne sat on the edge of Gail's bed, took her hand and asked if she was sure that marrying Arnold was what she wanted. Lillie and Wayne had discussed it, but Wayne was the better one to express things in words. If Lillie could not find the words when there were serious things to discuss with the girls, Wayne would do the talking.

"Don't let the fact that you have invited people to the wedding make you go through with it if you are not sure," he said to Gail. "If you're not sure, put it off for a little while. You can always get married later."

Wayne knew what Gail was getting into. He knew about the conversations with Ethel, the priest being so hard on her because she was not Catholic and the changes expected of her. Wayne coming to her room and talking with her meant a lot to Gail. She appreciated the love.

Lillie later said Wayne sobbed that night because he was not able to do more for both his girls. As the girls were growing up, he had made plans of things he would do for Darlene after Gail was married, which were now impossible. He also wished he had been able to do more for Gail. Lillie told him that he had given Gail something that money could not buy; something that would last forever.

Lillie and Wayne loved Arnold and accepted him as their son. When Ethel was telling Lillie that if Gail were her daughter, she would not let her marry Arnold, Lillie responded, "I think I know your son better than you do."

Arnold had been out of Escanaba and his parent's home since he joined the Air Force two years earlier. He had made his mistakes, and he was not the same boy who left home. He had grown from a boy to a young man, and Ethel was not with him during the change.

Choosing a time of day for the wedding was simple. Forenoon weddings were common because the couple was required to fast for twenty-four hours before the ceremony.

The morning of the wedding, a famished Gail rode to the small Catholic chapel on the airbase in a Lincoln Continental owned and driven by her Uncle Vawn, with his wife Pauline in the passenger seat. Lillie and Wayne were in the vehicle ahead of them, leading the way to the chapel. Vawn was a salesman and always had a nice car. He said his car was not only his office, it also was the first thing people saw, and first impressions were critical for a salesman.

About eight rows of wooden pews faced the altar of the small chapel on the base. To prevent Arnold from seeing her, Gail was put in the one confessional while he took care of some last minute details. Though Arnold could not see Gail, she watched him as he talked with the priest.

Being excited, tense or nervous always made walking more of challenge than normal for Gail. The morning of the wedding, Wayne thought he was going to have to pick her up and carry her down the aisle to give her away.

Handsome in his dark navy blue suit, with his Clark Gable smile and dark hair, Wayne offered his left arm to Gail as they made their way down the short aisle, close friends and relatives in the pews on either side. Wayne said he was dragging her.

Arnold, in his Air Force uniform, stood at the altar with Joe as the best man next to him, and a woman Gail barely knew as the maid of honor on the other side. The maid of honor was a friend of Arnold's whom he met at the airport. Because of the war, the Air Force had taken over the Wichita airport, and she worked for an airline at the ticket counter. She was chosen to be in the wedding because both of the witnesses needed to be members of the Catholic church.

Vows were exchanged, and Gail and Arnold were pronounced man and wife, and Arnold would not kiss her in front of everyone. Though Gail was unaware of what he was doing, Arnold said he wanted their first kiss as man and wife to be just theirs. He did not want to share it, but he also wanted it recorded. At Noon, the only person who saw their first kiss as husband and wife was Ernie Spriggs. He took the photos at the wedding and developed them in the darkroom at the Wichita Beacon newspaper office, where he worked.

Arnold and Gail on their wedding day, with Lillie and Wayne.

The couple got married on a three-day pass, so they spent their wedding night in their own apartment, though Lillie told everyone they were going to Kansas City. Arnold and Gail found the two-room basement apartment, at the corner of Douglas and Kansas streets, about three weeks earlier. They were lucky to find it, because rentable apartments were scarce.

The door to the apartment was to the right at the bottom of about seven stairs, and it opened up to a living room with pink and gray plaid walls that also doubled as the bedroom. The apartment included a kitchen and a bathroom, with a potbellied gas stove in the living room for heat.

The couple slept on a couch that flattened down to make a bed. Arnold was so tall he had to sleep at a diagonal on the bed because of the location of the arm rests. Eventually, they got a roll-away bed so they could sleep more comfortably.

Darlene and Ernie lived in the apartment next door. They had rented theirs before Arnold and Gail. Darlene heard about the apartment from a girl in school whose aunt owned the building. When Gail and Arnold heard about the other apartment being available and then rented it, Darlene was mad. "I got married to move away from you, and you follow me," she said.

Living next to each other as married women is where Gail and Darlene actually got to know each other. There was a door between the two apartments that had been boarded up and painted over. The couples unblocked it, giving the women the opportunity to enjoy each other's company as they did housework while the men worked second shift.

"We found out we really liked each other," said Gail.

With the limited use of her right hand and her slower reactions, Gail had never learned to drive a car, though she wanted to give it a try. Sure that she would be able to do it, Arnold set about teaching her.

Arnold and Gail, along with Lillie and Wayne, had driven out to Cheney to visit family. On the way home Arnold pulled the car over, deciding the quite gravel road was a good place for Gail to try driving for the first time. They switched places, and Gail settled in behind the wheel. The seat had to be adjusted in order for her short legs to reach the gasoline and brake pedals.

Arnold coached her through putting the car in drive and inching it back onto the road. As she sped up, she began weaving back and forth across the road, causing Lillie to squeal in the back seat. Gail could not get the car under control enough to move forward in a straight line.

It was like an amusement ride. Lillie kept squealing. Wayne told her to be quiet. Arnold was in the passenger seat trying to give Gail instructions, which seemed to fall on deaf ears. Gail said she heard the instructions, but her body just worked slower. When the car nearly went into the ditch, saved from that fate by Arnold grabbing the wheel, the driving session was over.

"I didn't catch on as Arnie thought I should," said Gail. Arnold thought her reaction time was too slow, and worried what would happen to her or the other people out on the road. That was the last lesson he gave her. Not wanting to worry Arnold, Gail never tried to drive a car again.

As Mrs. Arnold Johnson, Gail did not go back to college. Before marrying Arnold, Gail was working at the dance studio as a "girl Friday". After the wedding, she became the full-time receptionist, working 11 a.m. to 5 p.m. Both Arnold and Gail spent a lot of time at the studio, and Eileen enlisted Arnold's help with painting. Later he took on janitorial duties. Working for Eileen gave him a reason to be with Gail, and also gave the couple a little more money.

The three of them would talk about anything and everything during breaks in the afternoon, all of them having music in common. Music had been a part of Arnold's life growing up, both at home and school. He played several different instruments, and had a band when he graduated from high school. He also wrote arrangements of patriotic songs for Escanaba's city band.

It was during one of those afternoon chats at the dance studio that the idea of handicapped dance classes was born. Gail asked Eileen if she had ever considered teaching handicapped ballroom dancing, using things like marching instead of stepping so people would not drag their feet. Eileen loved the idea and asked if Arnold and Gail would like to teach the class.

They accepted the challenge, and one hour a week, for about nine months, Arnold and Gail taught eight to ten people with a variety of disabilities how to dance. The majority of the students were people Gail had known from the Institute of Logopedics.

Arnold also accompanied Gail to the Handicap Plus club meetings where he became friends with many handicapped people. He called one of the women, who had more severe cerebral palsy than Gail, an "amazing" woman. She had a great sense of humor and was a joy to be around. He could not figure out why she was single. "Some man is really missing out," he told Gail.

∞

Attending college was not easy for Mom. There were no ramps or elevators, making some of what we consider simple tasks much harder. Every day Mom went down three flights of stairs in her home, walked half a block, and went up another 20 concrete stairs before she was even in the building. She then went up additional stairs to get to her classes. Moving forward and not quitting were already ingrained in the fabric of her being, though she said her grades were not very good because she "was having too much fun."

The process of Mom and Dad getting married also was not easy, but Dad would not quit. He was a man who at one time could not stand to be around handicapped people, yet he fell in love with Mom before he even noticed her handicap. By then, it was too late, and he knew he wanted to spend the rest of his life with her. She was worth all the trouble.

Through being around Mom, Dad learned that handicapped people are just people. Some are ornery and cranky, some are sweet and kind, and some have a wonderful sense of humor. Their personalities are as individual and unique as able-bodied people. Accomplishing things just takes them a little longer.

CHAPTER 6

⸎

Having Children

Before the wedding, Arnold and Gail knew they wanted to raise a family, but having children right away was out of the question. Shortly after their first anniversary, they decided it best to talk to a doctor to see if it was wise for Gail to get pregnant. The doctor said he could see no reason why not, so they changed their strategy from stopping a pregnancy to starting one.

In September, 1956, Arnold received an honorable discharge from the Air Force. The couple was still living in the two-room basement apartment on Douglas Street, and he took a job with the county treasurer for Sedgwick County. The county treasurer, a small, kind woman, was good at her job, which included selling car tabs and running the licensing bureau. She hired Arnold as a clerk in the license bureau, and also allowed him to make extra money by selling lists of who bought what model of cars. Selling those lists was legal at the time, and car companies, as well as others, used them for marketing.

A couple of months later, Gail became pregnant with their first child. She waited to tell Arnold until she was almost sure she was pregnant, and then slipped the fact into a conversation while they were talking about a friend's pregnancy.

"I think I am, too," she told Arnold.

Excitement filled Arnold, but Gail still needed to do a pregnancy test with a doctor, which took two weeks. A lab technician would inject the woman's urine into a live rabbit, and if the rabbit died, the woman was pregnant. The rabbit did die, signaling the new life growing inside Gail.

Darlene, who had already given birth to a boy and was pregnant with a second child, referred Gail to her doctor, Dr. Charles Mitchell. He took a special interest in Gail, partly because he had a seven-year-old boy who also had cerebral Palsy.

The pregnancy was hard on Gail, with her small frame and spastic body. She was not built to have children, and she spent a lot of time at the doctor's office. Dr. Mitchell's gentle features and kind disposition were a comfort when she was having trouble. Because Gail had been in the office so often, he told her she had enough problems to have given birth to six children.

The next spring, Arnold and Gail moved to a bigger place on 9th Street. It was an unfurnished duplex apartment with four rooms—living room, bedroom, kitchen and bathroom, with glass French doors between the living room and bedroom. They borrowed a bed from Wayne and Lillie, bought a daybed couch for the living room and had a card table and chairs in the kitchen. They also got a bassinet and began collecting things for the baby. Lillie said she had never seen a more pregnant man than Arnold.

Arnold was itching to get back to working with airplanes. He had been an air traffic controller in the Air Force, which is why the Air Force did not send him overseas to Korea. The government felt his job was too important and needed to be done on United States soil.

Arnold loved anything associated with airplanes—controlling air traffic, piloting small airplanes, going to air shows, etc. Though not yet certified, his goal was to become a pilot for his own recreation and transportation, which happened many years later. The lessons and putting in the flight time to get the license were expensive, so he had to wait.

Arnold applied to the Civil Aeronautics Association, the governing agency for non-military air traffic controllers. In April, he was told to report to St. Joseph, Missouri, to begin a job as an air traffic controller at Rosecrans Memorial Airport. Because of the pregnancy, Arnold was given time before he had to report to work, but when June rolled around, his supervisor said to report to the airport or he would lose the job. The job was important to him, but so was his family. He did not want to miss the delivery of the baby.

The couple asked Dr. Mitchell if there would be enough time for Arnold to get back to Wichita from St. Joe when Gail went into labor.

"You should have enough time," he said. "The labor usually is longer with the first one. But if I have to do a cesarean section, I want you back three days before, so you two can have some quality time together before the baby is born."

That was the first time the doctor mentioned a C-section birth. Once a woman had one C-section, the rest of her children would be born the same way because of a concern that a previous C-section incision could split during a natural birth, causing internal bleeding.

Though it was hard to leave, Arnold went to St. Joe, renting a room in an upstairs apartment that he shared with several other men who were bachelors. Gail moved in with Lillie and Wayne so she could continue her prenatal care in Wichita.

Gail never saw Arnold's apartment in the old river town because he refused to take her there. He said the other men would bring home "loose women" and he did not want to subject her to those situations. The apartment also was on the top floor of an old building that did not have an elevator, and he felt there were too many stairs for her to climb.

Though Gail was still working at the dance studio, it was getting to be too much for her. She took time off toward the end of the pregnancy, and spent the majority of her time resting.

Her due date came and went, with no contractions. She had gained seventeen pounds, which was a good amount for her small frame. A baby grows so fast after the due date, which concerned Dr. Mitchell. A week later, the decision was made to take the baby via a C-section. Dr. Mitchell did not want to be faced with making the decision of who would live, the mother or the baby.

"Gail, don't do that to me," he said. "Let's take it (the baby) and have a healthy baby and a healthy mother."

Dr. Mitchell set the date for July 12, 1957, and he insisted that Arnold get back to Wichita in time to spend a few days with Gail before the surgery, which Gail later said should have been an indication to her that he expected problems.

Gail reported to the Osteopathic Hospital the afternoon before the scheduled C-section so tests could be done to make sure everything was on track. Arnold spent the afternoon with her as she was stripped of her street clothes and put in one of those hospital gowns that are open in the back. Then the nurses poked and prodded Gail for the tests. Arnold stayed as late as the hospital would allow, kissed Gail good night and told her he would see her in the morning.

The plan was for Arnold to be with Gail through the surgery, though she was going to be asleep under the anesthetics. When he got back in the morning, the hospital could not find booties large enough to fit over his size thirteen shoes. If they had allowed Arnold in the operating room, one static spark caused by his shoes could have killed everyone in the room. Arnold stood in the doorway, eyes locked with Gail's as the anesthetics took hold. His face was the last thing she saw as she went to sleep.

Waiting in the room down the hall, Arnold, Lillie and Wayne prayed that everything would go well.

A girl with dark hair and inquisitive eyes came into the world later that day. Arnold and Gail named her Ethel Lucille Johnson, after both grandmothers. Gail thought Lillie's middle name was Lucille and later realized it was Lucinda. Arnold called the baby his "little princess" and purchased her a doll dressed as a bride.

After the surgery, Arnold was allowed to sit with Gail in the recovery room. Gail was not doing well. It took a while for her to come out of the anesthetics, and as she woke, she saw him sitting on a chair near her, his head laying on his arm on the bed. As he saw her eyes open, he gently pushed on the bed to stand up and bent over to kiss her.

He called a nurse, and they brought Gail something to eat, which was a mistake. She was so sick, they ended up having to pump her stomach. The next few days were no better. On the third day, she was so close to death that Arnold called the family in to say their good-byes. Gail can remember her Uncle Charlie standing at the end of the bed shaking his head as he said, "It's a shame. It's a shame."

"Well, how does it feel to be a new mother?" Dr. Mitchell asked as he walked in the room, trying to lighten the atmosphere.

"I don't know. I haven't seen my baby yet," said Gail. Everyone had been so concerned about her, they forgot to show her the beautiful baby girl.

"Oh my! We will take care of that right now," he said as he headed to the nursery. When he showed her the little bundle of joy, he told her she was healthy and that she had all ten fingers and toes.

Until the crisis was over, Arnold never left Gail's side, except to go to the bathroom. The nurses brought him food and water, and allowed him to help take care of her.

As the days wore on, Gail gradually got better. She and the baby, whom they decided to call Lucille, were in the hospital ten days. Arnold had to go back to St. Joe before they were released, but until he left, he spent every waking minute at the hospital — the nurses allowing him to break the visiting hour rules. He would help tend to Gail's needs, even helping bathe her. After Arnold had left for St. Joe, a nurse told Gail that all of the nurses wished they had a man like him.

When they left the hospital, Gail and Lucille went to stay with Wayne and Lillie at their house on South Falustia Street, so Gail would have help. A dining room in their small rented home had been converted to Gail's bedroom. She was recovering slowly, and the girdle she was prescribed to wear was too difficult for Gail to put on herself. Wayne, with his strong hands, helped her with that, which was embarrassing for Gail.

"Don't be silly," he said. "I diapered you a long time ago."

Handling children was not new to Gail. She had babysat for several different families as a teen-ager. To pick up the baby, she would grab one of the baby's arms with her left hand, lift the baby and then wrap her right arm around the baby's body. Lillie worried that the little one would end up with one arm longer than the other, but the doctor reassured her that would not happen.

"Don't worry. The baby is used to it," he said. "Babies are not as delicate as people might think."

Changing a diaper was a little challenging, but Gail figured out a system that worked. She was lucky, both her daughters were calm babies who did a pretty good job of holding still while she clipped the diaper pins. She did not have to get after them very often to hold still.

For three months, Arnold and Gail lived apart, which was hard on both of them. Arnold missed out on precious time with his wife and new baby, and made the trip to Wichita as often as possible.

On one of his visits to Wichita, Gail and Arnold wanted some time alone. Arnold asked Lillie to watch Lucille while they went to a drive-in movie.

"No. That's your baby. You take care of her," she told him.

After Gail was feeling better, she went back to the dance studio for a couple of hours in the afternoons while Lillie watched Lucille.

In the fall, just before their third anniversary, Gail and Lucille joined Arnold in St. Joe. They moved into a furnished apartment upstairs in a huge old house that still had the wide woodwork and hardwood floors. Though the house had been converted into an apartment building, their five rooms—living room, dining room, bedroom, bathroom and kitchen—were spacious.

The Rosecrans Memorial Airport is located on a piece of land cut off from St. Joe by the Great Flood of 1951, which changed the course of the Missouri River. To get to work, Arnold had to cross the river into Kansas and cross it again to get back into Missouri. When the river flooded, he had to drive south and cross the river at Leavenworth, Kansas, drive north again, and finally cross the river near the airport.

Gail busied herself turning their apartment into a home and taking care of Lucille. She stopped participating in telethons for the Institute of Logopedics, but she continued doing presentations by telling her story, and also volunteering. She met Rosemary Purcell, who became a good friend, while volunteering at a nursery for handicapped children. Rosemary's daughter had cerebral palsy and learned to do everything, which included eating, with her feet.

Rosemary was one of Gail's greatest advocates, and helped her connect with the right groups for her presentations. She loved sharing Gail's story with her friends. When friend Marge Miner, who had a daytime TV talk show, heard about Gail, she asked her to appear on the show. Miner received the Golden Mic Award for that episode, and a photograph of Miner and Gail appeared in McCall's, a national women's magazine. Arnold could not have been more thrilled.

Though Gail was told she should not have any more children, she and Arnold wanted one more. They had planned on waiting until Lucille was three years old, but God had other ideas. Gail got pregnant with her second child shortly after their fourth wedding anniversary, when Lucille was just past her first birthday. When they realized Gail was pregnant again, they both sat on the edge of the bed and cried.

Having been in St. Joe such a short time, Gail was not sure where to find a doctor. She went to Rosemary for advice.

"I don't know any doctors here," she said.

"Don't be silly," Rosemary laughed. Gail, dressed in a black felt skirt and peach blouse, had recently given a presentation to a roomful of doctors at a medical association meeting. One of those doctors would surely work.

Gail ended up with a doctor who had a fourteen-year-old son with cerebral palsy. Part of the deal was that Arnold would take the boy to the air traffic control tower.

"God sent me to the right doctors each time," Gail said.

On their first visit, Arnold and Gail told him they had no insurance; and that they were living paycheck to paycheck. They were not sure when they would be able to pay, and they wanted him to know that before he took their case.

"Don't worry about it," he said. "You won't receive any bills. Just take care of it as you can."

They started paying ten dollars here and ten dollars there so the final bill would not be as much, and soon they began receiving bills. When Gail told the doctor, he excused himself from the examination room for a little while.

"Leave those kids alone!" he told the business office. "If necessary, I will pay the bill."

Gail's body struggled even more during the second pregnancy than the first. She was sick most of the time, and unable to keep anything down. She gained only four pounds over the entire pregnancy, though she delivered an eight-pound baby.

Being so sick, she needed help with the house work and care of Lucille. Working rotating shifts, there were some weeks when Arnold was home during the day. Those weeks were not the problem. It was the other weeks, when Gail was home alone all day, that were getting difficult for her.

"I need to go home to Mom and Dad," she begged. "I can't take it, being so sick."

"You're not going home," said Arnold. He wanted to be with Gail during the end of the pregnancy and after the baby's birth. "I missed it with Lucille. I'm not missing it with this one."

"But I can't do it!" Gail said.

"You're not going!" Arnold replied.

It did not end there. Gail was so serious about going to Wichita, she had a neighbor stay with Lucille while she discussed the situation with an attorney. She needed to know where she stood legally if she left, and if there was a chance she could lose Lucille by choosing to go to her parents.

At Gail's next doctor's visit, she said nothing about the conflict. She kept the conversation with the doctor about the pregnancy. After the visit, the doctor called Arnold and said, "You have to get her some help. Either send her home to her parents or get her some help. I don't want her doing one dish!"

"What did you tell him?" Arnold later asked in an accusatorial tone.

"I didn't say a word," replied Gail.

Rather than sending her away, he got on the phone to his mother in Escanaba and asked if his fifteen-year-old sister, Barb, could come to Missouri for the summer to help. It was the end of the school year, and the baby was due before school was to start in the fall.

Ethel left the decision up to Barb, who got excited at the prospect of going to St. Joe. Barb packed a bag and, accompanied by Ethel, caught the train from Escanaba to Omaha, Nebraska, where Arnold retrieved her.

That summer, Arnold enlisted the help of men who worked with him at the control tower to move the family's few possessions into half of a duplex, making things easier for Gail. The stairs to the apartment were getting too difficult for her to navigate with one baby in her arms and another in her tummy. The furnished duplex had large rooms, with a small sunken patio out the back door, giving Gail a convenient place for Lucille to play outside. A gate was placed at the bottom of the stairs leading to the yard and Lucille could play on the patio without Gail having to chase her around.

The duplex also had a basement that Arnold and Gail could use, which is where Arnold set up his photography darkroom. It was the first place they lived where the bathroom did not double as a darkroom.

After moving everything into the new place, including a day bed purchased for Barb to use as a bed, Arnold went to work the evening shift, leaving the girls alone. Later when Lucille was asleep, and Gail and Barb were getting ready for bed, Gail in her thy-length nightgown and Barb in her pajamas, an enormous water bug ran across the living room floor, scaring the two of them. The teenager and pregnant woman bolted up onto the day bed, where they were jumping up and down squealing when Arnold got home.

Helping with cooking, cleaning and taking care of Lucille was not the hard part for Barb. The hard part was when Gail would fall, which she often did. That really scared Barb. She was afraid both for Gail and the baby.

The doctor told Barb not to worry about the baby because Gail's body would shelter it. She was told only to worry about Gail.

"I didn't realize how sturdy babies really are," said Barb.

By the mid-1950s, the national civil rights movement had gained momentum. Bus boycotts, marches and sit-in protests were taking place all over the south. Organizations were cropping up all over the country to combat discrimination, some peaceful and some violent.

In Wichita, Gail had grown up side-by-side with minorities, sitting next to them in school. Desegregation of schools confused her because the schools she attended already were mixed. If minorities were receiving substandard education, so was she.

Though Missouri and Kansas were considered part of the North at the time, there were still segregated schools, restaurants, etc. In Topeka, Kansas, a parent sued the school board to allow his eight-year-old daughter to attend a school that was near their home, rather than ride the bus one mile to the "colored" school. By the time the courts settled the case, others had joined. The 1950 decision to allow the child to go to the local school affected school segregation all across the nation.

Growing up in Escanaba, Barb had not been exposed to segregated lunch counters, or "whites only" restrooms and drinking fountains. In 1959, even though Missouri was not as segregated as states in the deep south, it was still a culture shock for her. The disparity between facilities and the discrimination because of skin color appalled her.

During her stay with Gail and Arnold, Barb and the friends she made in St. Joe staged a sit-in protest at a local segregated lunch counter.

As the baby's due date grew closer, Rosemary took Mom to the small Catholic hospital on 9ᵗʰ Street, about three blocks from the duplex, to meet some of the nuns. She thought it would make it easier for Arnold and Gail when it came time to deliver the baby.

While talking with one of the Sisters, Gail told her they did not have insurance, or money for that matter.

"What is wrong with you people?" one Sister snapped at Gail. "You know that in nine months you are going to have a baby. Why don't you save money?"

That comment hurt Gail's feelings. Arnold and she were doing the best they could.

"Don't feel bad," said Rosemary. "She has no concept of what it's like on the outside."

Arnold was not happy when she told him what happened. He went to the credit union and borrowed money to pay for the birth ahead of time.

"Why did you do that?" the doctor asked when he found out. "I could have fixed it up for you. Now it's too late."

Gail was admitted into the hospital on Aug. 23, with the C-section birth scheduled for the next day. Wayne and Lillie left Wichita heading for St. Joe to be there when the baby was born. After tests had been done, the doctors decided the baby was not ready. They wanted to give it one more week of growth, so they sent Gail back home.

Cell phones were not yet invented, so there was no way to notify Lillie and Wayne of the delay until they arrived. Lillie stayed, and Wayne headed back to Wichita after a couple of days, planning to return.

A week later, Gail started having contractions. Wayne sat at her bedside holding her hand, and Arnold called from work every few minutes to see how things were going. Instead of taking the time off of work before the birth, he was saving as much time as he could save for after the birth.

The following morning, Arnold was with Gail as she prepared for surgery; though this time, he was not given the option to be with her in the operating room during the birth. The anesthesiologist gave a spinal tap, which made her numb from the waist down, and the couple exchanged kisses and said "I love you" as she was wheeled into the operating room.

Gail Arlene Johnson, a flaming red-hair little girl, was born on Aug. 31, 1959, with Arnold, Lillie and Wayne waiting near the elevator on the maternity floor. Barb and Lucille anxiously awaited news at home.

The surgery went much smoother than the first birth, and Gail was able to see the baby before the nurse took her to be cleaned up. As the nurse stepped out of the elevator on the maternity floor, she handed the baby to Arnold, who showed her to Lillie and Wayne before taking her to the nursery.

When she was ready, Gail was transferred from the operating recovery room to a hospital room that she shared with one other woman, though Gail had a private nurse. Being married to one of the air traffic controllers who worked with Arnold, the nurse shared a bond with Gail and took her on as her only patient.

The hospital was a teaching hospital, which meant its students and interns routinely took care of daily tasks. The nurse who watched over Gail did not want anyone else to take care of her, and would get upset when the staff would give her shots or medicine before she arrived in the morning. She knew the trouble Gail had with Lucille's birth and wanted the best for her this time around.

The bright red hair, which matched neither of the parents, tickled the funny bones of many people who came to visit. They teased Gail, saying there must have been a milk man somewhere in the picture.

A couple of days after Gail Arlene's birth, Ethel took the train to Omaha, where Arnold collected her. She was not staying long as her mission had another element. She needed to get Barb back to Escanaba in time for the start of the school year.

When Ethel arrived at the hospital, the nurse broke the rules and let her hold the baby, knowing it was the only time she would see her before heading back home.

With Barb on her way back to Escanaba and Wayne heading back to Wichita, Arnold went back to work. He was saving his time off for a few weeks down the line when Lillie needed to get back to Wichita.

Recovery went well for Gail, but it was difficult to find a formula the baby could keep down. Though mom and baby were sent home about eight days after the birth, Gail Arlene was still vomiting up most of whatever they fed her. Arnold said she was a happy baby, even though she was so sick. They tried every type of formula they could find, but her body would accept none of them. Finally, the doctor suggested whole cows milk, and it worked. Gail Arlene was drinking whole cows milk from the time she was a few weeks old.

Gail and Arnold with their children.

Arnold originally wanted a large family. Being the oldest of five, he helped raise his siblings and loved the idea of filling his house with children. All that changed after Gail Arlene was born. With Gail on her death bed after Lucille's birth and being so sick during the pregnancy with Gail Arlene, he decided they were done.

The Catholic church was against birth control, stating that children were a blessing from God and people should have as many children as possible. It also stated that if the pregnancy was threatening the life of the mother, the family should continue the pregnancy and leave it as God wills. If the mother was to die, the father could always find another woman to mother the children.

"Honey, it doesn't work that way," Arnold told Gail. "My children need their mother more than they need another sibling. And I need you."

∞

I was the last child my mother gave birth to. Some people thought she should never have children, and wondered why she would even want them; to which Mom has always replied that handicapped people have the same needs and desires as everyone else.

It may have been harder for her to have children than most women, it was harder for her to walk across the floor, too. Mom did not quit just because life is hard. She does not define life by how easy it is to do things. She defines life by how important the tasks are.

"It takes a lot of living to make a life," she says. "For someone who was not supposed to be any more than a vegetable, I have done a lot."

CHAPTER 7

Family Life

Gail and Arnold had trouble making ends meet financially. They were still paying on the hospital bill from Lucille's birth, plus the credit union payments from Gail Arlene's birth. Add to that the living expenses for a family of four and the paycheck at the tower was not enough. To supplement their income, Arnold took on some odd jobs, which included collecting money from pop and music vending machines, and doing electrical work for friends.

It was a difficult time, especially for Gail. Being alone with the children so much was hard, and she missed precious time with Arnold.

Gail continued volunteering at the nursery, taking both children along. She said being around the handicapped children was good for them, and it also was good for the other children.

The opportunity for Arnold to advance in his field came in 1961. He was transferred to the only civilian operated control tower at a U.S. Air Force Strategic Air Command Base, located in Lincoln, Nebraska. By the time he received the transfer, the name of the government department overseeing air traffic controllers had changed from the Civil Aeronautics Administration to the Federal Aviation Agency (FAA). In January, Gail and Arnold packed everything they owned into a station wagon, including their two daughters, and made the 130-mile trip to Lincoln.

While entering the city, a police officer, who was looking for a stolen shipment of sweaters, pulled them over. Someone had taken sweaters from a local department store, and the packed station wagon looked suspicious.

"That was our introduction to Lincoln," Gail said.

Arnold had already found a house to rent a couple of blocks from the capital building, but it was too late at night to meet with the landlord. The family spent its first night in the new city in a hotel room, which is where Gail Arlene decided it was time to be potty trained.

Gail was going to wait until Gail Arlene was two years old before training her, but in the middle of the move, when she was eighteen months old, she went all night with a dry diaper. Gail told Arnold she was ready to train. Watching Lucille use the little yellow potty chair that looked like the big toilet Mom and Dad used clinched the deal. Gail Arlene potty trained overnight, which made life much easier for Gail. She had been washing cloth diapers since Lucille was born, sometimes having to wash them by hand.

The next day, the family moved into a house built at the end of the 1800s that still sported the character of the original construction. There were pillars on top of one-quarter walls between the dining room and the living room, and plain wide woodwork throughout the house.

Instead of a basement, the house had a cellar one could enter through a doorway in the kitchen or outside through angled double doors. The outside cellar doors were at just the right angle for Lucille to use as a slide.

Gail and Arnold took the large bedroom at the end of the hall and put the girls in the bedroom off the dining room. They purchased a twin bed for Lucille and set up a crib for Gail Arlene.

Living in the middle of Lincoln was a good location for both Gail and Arnold. From the house to the air base was a fifteen-minute commute, and the house was in walking distance of many different stores, shops and services, making it easy for Gail to take care of daily activities. She had a stroller with a removable seat that turned into a walker. She would push one child in the stroller, and the other child held onto it while walking alongside.

The girls learned early that they did not run from Gail. Arnold would not allow it, and they behaved well when he was around. Gail said they just understood that they could not run from her.

One of the places Gail liked to walk to was Sears, about eight blocks away from the house. It had a photography studio that often ran specials on children's portraits. During one of those specials, which Gail could not pass up, she dressed the girls in pretty little dresses and walked the eight blocks to get pictures taken. When she got home, Arnold had an insurance agent at the house, talking about life insurance. The agent was hesitant to insure Gail because of her handicap.

As he was leaving, the agent noticed the stroller in the yard that Gail had forgotten to put back on the porch. He asked about it, and she told him she had just taken the girls to Sears to get pictures taken. With eyebrows lifted and a surprised look on his face, he said "If you can do that, you are insurable."

Being new in town, Gail and Arnold were looking for ways to get to know people. Arnold joined a FAA bowling league with some of the men he worked with at the control tower. While he bowled, Gail watched, sitting in the back with the children in tow.

A woman noticed Mom and asked why she was not bowling.

"Arnie thought I might hurt myself."

"Do you want to bowl?" she asked.

"Yes," replied Gail.

A few days later Gail received a call letting her know she had been added as the sixth bowler on a four-member team in a women's league.

"Do the ladies know I am handicapped and have never bowled before?" Gail asked.

"Yes. We want you," was the reply.

When Arnold got home from work, Gail told him about the phone call, and said she planned on bowling in the women's league.

"I guess if you're going to be bowling, maybe I should show you how to do it," he said.

He took her to the local lanes during open bowling, showed her how to choose a bowling ball to fit her fingers and at a weight she could manage. She would pick up her bowling ball with her left hand, hold it in the elbow of her right arm, limp up to the line and then swing her left arm and release the ball.

He told her it was necessary to keep her shoulders as straight as possible, and square with the line. He also worked with her on her swing, telling her to keep her eye on the mark over which she wanted the ball to roll.

When Gail started bowling, she carried a thirty-four-pin average. By the time she stopped bowling thirty years later, she carried an average in the 120s and had bowled three games over 200 points.

"The ladies put up with me, all except one," said Gail. The woman said Gail could not bowl on the league because she did not have an approach.

Arnold begged to differ. "She couldn't get to the line if she didn't have an approach," he said.

A local sports writer spotted Gail on one of his visits during league bowling. He watched for a while, and returned at another time to talk with her. When Gail readily agreed to an interview, he asked about her handicap, and how she got started bowling. He wrote up a feature article about her for the sports section.

"I never dreamed I would be written up in a sports section," said Gail.

While in Lincoln, Gail began learning the basics of bowling from Arnold, and Arnold began learning the value of having pets from Gail. He had grown up with a dog tied to a dog house in the back yard. The dog was an animal, not a pet. He was of the opinion that animals belonged out in the yard, not in the house.

Gail's view was very different. Animals had always played an important role in her life, and had been wonderful companions. It took a long time to convince him that they should have a pet, and he finally relented. He gave permission for a kitten, and went to get one.

A cat has an innate ability to know when someone does not like it, often making that person the focus of its affection, or condescension. Arnold and the little white kitten with black spots did not hit it off well. They fought in the car all the way home. By the time Arnold brought the kitten into the kitchen through the back door, scratches stretched from his hand all the way up his arm.

He threw the little creature onto the kitchen floor as he yelled, "If that cat so much as scratches one of the girls, out it goes."

To get away from Arnold, the kitten ran behind the television set where it stayed until Lucille wiggled into the small space to bring it out. As she emerged with the kitten in her arms, it was purring as if it had known her all its life.

Getting up from her nap, Gail Arlene toddled into the kitchen and sat on the floor, rubbing the sleepiness from her eyes. The kitten trotted over to her, tail in the air, and started rubbing against her purring.

The family named the kitten Kitty-Purr after Gail Arlene's stuffed cat, which got its name after a visit from Darlene. She had lifted the stuffed kitten in her cupped hands, bringing it nose to nose with her, encouraging it to purr. "Kitty, purr. Kitty, purr."Arnold's heart softened as Kitty-Purr began to wiggle his way into the family's life.

At least once a year, Arnold and Gail would pack the girls, luggage, picnic lunches and Kitty-Purr into the car, and drive the fourteen-hour, 730-mile trip to Escanaba. Arnold liked to drive straight through, only stopping to eat and go to the bathroom. When stopping for picnic breaks along the way, they never needed a leash for Kitty-Purr. He would jump out of the car with everyone else, run around the picnic grounds climbing trees and checking out the local flora and fauna, and then be right beside the car when it was time to leave.

At Escanaba, Arnold's family welcomed Gail with open arms, with the exception of Ethel. She never warmed up to her.

Three of Arnold's siblings—Jim, Don and Barb—gradually moved from Escanaba, taking up residence in and around Milwaukee, Wisconsin. The trips soon alternated between visiting family in Escanaba, Milwaukee and Wichita.

Working as an air traffic controller, Arnold was working rotating shifts, which meant he often slept during the day. On those days, Gail was charged with keeping the little ones as quiet as possible.

Nearly a year after the family moved in to the house in Lincoln, the landlord put the house up for sale. He wanted to have a chance to talk with Gail and Arnold before anyone looked at the property, but there was a miscommunication with the realtor. The realtor sent a couple over to see the house unannounced. Arnold was on night rotation, and was sleeping when the couple knocked on the door.

"There will be no more of that!" Arnold said. He was not going to have his sleep disturbed again, nor have their next home sold out from under them. He searched for a house they could afford on his airport pay, and found a small one in a new neighborhood near the University of Nebraska's experimental fields, on the northwest side of Lincoln,.

Arnold and Gail purchased a newly constructed rambler on Seward Avenue for $11,200. It had two bedrooms, a bathroom, a living room and a kitchen on the main level, and an unfinished basement.

The house was set back from the curb, leaving a decent sized front yard, and the treeless back yard stretched to the dirt alley that separated the yard from a railroad track on top of a large berm. The dirt alley led to the university's fields about a half-block away.

As part of the down payment, Gail and Arnold painted walls and finished the windows. They ended up with monthly house payments of eighty-nine dollars. The next spring, they set about planting grass and trees in the yard, and added a swing set for the children.

A washer and dryer was installed in the basement, and a clothes line was put up in the back yard. As time went on, Arnold framed in a bedroom, work room and bathroom in the basement. The work room had a long wooden work bench that he used for a lot of different projects around the house. It also was as a place to experiment with electronics, and he constructed a ham radio.

Moving to Seward Avenue doubled the commuting time to get to the airport, but that did not matter. Pleased to have a home of his own, Arnold also appreciated the added security that his family could be there as long as they wanted. No one could sell it out from under them.

Being so far from the middle of town made things a little more difficult for Gail. She no longer had the freedom to walk to the store to get things, or walk to the beauty shop to have her hair done. She had to plan things around Arnold's work schedule so he could take her.

Kitty-Purr loved the new house and enjoyed the freedom of mouse hunting in the nearby fields. He often would be gone for the entire day and come home relaxed and happy.

The other residents in the new neighborhood welcomed the family with open arms. Everyone was at about the same economic level, and the majority of the women were stay-at-home moms. The children in a two-block radius were about the same age, and they all played together. The moms organized a weekly coffee group where they would talk while the children played.

A German couple, Fred and Gerta, owned the house next door. They were older than Gail and Arnold, but the four of them became great friends. One spring, soon after Gerta had planted the flowerbeds and Fred put grass seed in the yard, some of the flowers were uprooted. Fred got very angry and accused Lucille of yanking them out. Gail and Arnold took Lucille over to Fred and Gerta's house to talk, and Lucille kept claiming she was innocent. She said maybe it was Gail Arlene.

That made Fred pop a cork, and he said Lucille was lying. "Sweet little Gail wouldn't do something like that. It had to be Lucille," he said.

"If Lucille says she didn't do it, she didn't," said Arnold. "Lucille does not lie."

He headed over to their house, telling Fred and Gerta to wait a minute. He found Gail Arlene sitting on her twin bed in the room she shared with Lucille, waiting for him. He paraded her over to the neighbor's house, where she confessed to pulling up the plants.

Gerta requested Gail Arlene come back the next day and replant them, to which Gail and Arnold readily agreed. Once Gail Arlene got the flowers replanted, she walked across the freshly seeded yard. The first grass to poke up from the ground was in the shape of tiny footprints.

Later that summer, Gerta told Gail she should have Gail Arlene pull up all of her flowers and replant them. The ones that she replanted were growing the best.

The only time Kitty-Purr scratched a child was when Darlene and Ernie's two children, Cindy, who was about the same age as Lucille, and Wayne, who was about a year older, stayed with the family for a couple of weeks while Darlene was having surgery.

It was before Arnold framed the rooms in the basement, leaving a large space to play. The four children were taking turns riding a tricycle, and one of them had the bright idea of putting Kitty-Purr in the wire basket on the front and taking him for a ride. He got stuck in the basket, and his tail got caught in the front wheel of the tricycle.

Arnold bolted down the stairs when he heard the cat's yowl, finding Lucille and Cindy with scratches all over their arms and legs. He somehow got Kitty-Purr dislodged and the cat took off as fast as it could. Lucille and Cindy had to be taken to the doctor.

Kitty-Purr's life was cut short, by what no one knows for sure. Gail talked Arnold into taking one of the kittens from a litter at a neighbor's house down the street. They brought home another white and black kitten, though it had more black spots than Kitty-Purr.

Poncho, as he was named, was a particularly unusual kitten. He loved to sleep in boxes, of any size. As long as he could get his feet into the box, that is all that mattered. He also loved water. Gail said he forgot to read the chapter about water in the cat manual. He would run through the sprinkler with the neighborhood children, and would jump in the kiddy pool with them. He even jumped into the bathtub during bubble baths. All one could see was his eyes staring up through the bubbles.

Poncho did read the chapter in the manual about hunting, and loved to bring his catches home, which is how Lucille and Gail Arlene started learning about life, death and animal survival instincts. Poncho caught a small rabbit in the back yard while Lucille and Gail Arlene were playing. He was playing with it, as cats often do, letting it go and catching it again. The state of the scared, squealing rabbit made Lucille terribly upset.

When Poncho decided he had played enough, which only took a few minutes, he grabbed the rabbit and went in for the kill. That is when Lucille, with tears cascading down her cheeks, ran after Poncho screaming at him to let the bunny go.

Gail came out of the house and told her to stop. She sat down with the girls to talk about Poncho's instinct to kill the bunny for food. It was hard as they watched Poncho kill the poor little bunny, but it may have already been hurt beyond recovery. It was a difficult lesson that took time for Lucille to get over.

Gail took a break from public speaking while in Lincoln. She kept busy taking care of children, meeting with the neighborhood women, being co-leader of the neighborhood Blue Birds troop, playing cards with Arnold and other couples, and bowling.

In 1964, Gail got the news that her grandfather, William Buttel, died at the age of eighty-three years old. When Gail was a teenager, William and Ada left the home place in Milton and moved to William's home town, Hope, Kansas to take care of his father. William worked at a hardware store, and then owned a general store on Main Street, west of 2nd Street. Gail and Darlene would ride the train from Wichita to visit.

On Saturday nights, after William took the girls to a movie at the small movie theater on Main Street, he walked them to the drug store for an ice cream sundae, though he would never have one himself. He told the girls he would have his sundae tomorrow, on Sunday.

When he died, Gail headed to Hope for the funeral, leaving the rest of the family in Lincoln.

William's death was hard on everybody, especially Ada. They had been married about 65 years, and William truly loved her. When looking at the photograph in the paper announcing their 50th anniversary, he said, "The picture there is not the woman I slept with last night." He still saw her the way she looked when they fell in love.

Wayne's first response was to change his clothes, get a shovel and head outside to dig the grave, though he was in Wichita and his father in Hope. He was in shock, and Lillie had to sit him down and talk with him for quite a while.

Before the funeral, Darlene and Gail were in the mortuary with Ada, where they witnessed her taking William's face in her two hands, kissing him and asking "Why didn't you stay with me just a little bit longer, just a little bit longer?"

Ada died about three years later, and Gail did not go to the funeral. "I was too much of a coward to go to Grandma's funeral," she said. "I didn't want to see her in a casket."

National and world affairs were going through a lot of changes. Shortly after Gail and Arnold got married, the United States became more involved in Vietnam. The First Indochina War had ended. After a two-year truce between North and South Vietnam, the country was to be reunified and elections held. Advisors were sent to South Vietnam from the United States in the hopes of setting up a western-friendly government. Things did not go as planned. The country was not reunified, and the elections that were to take place in 1956 never happened.

By the early 1960s, the involvement of the United States military escalated, with the number of troops sent to South Vietnam tripling in 1961 and again in 1962. There were people across the U.S. who believed it critical that communists did not gain a foothold in South Vietnam, and an equal number of people who believed the United States had no business sending troops.

Then, in 1963, President John F. Kennedy was assassinated on a parade route through Houston, Texas, which shocked the world. Arnold was at work when it happened, and Gail was at the beauty shop having her hair done. The president's death dropped a cloak of sadness over the country.

Lyndon B. Johnson was sworn into office as the president, and he was challenged in the elections in 1964 by Arizona Senator Barry Goldwater. Johnson won with more than 60 percent of the popular vote, and electoral votes of 44 of the 50 states, plus the District of Columbia.

Johnson advocated social welfare programs, like Social Security, which began in the 1930s. During his presidency, more social welfare programs were implemented, including Medicare, Medicaid and the War on Poverty in 1965.

That same year, protests against the war escalated. People fled to Canada, dodging the draft.

The 1960s also was an era of social unrest and change in the United States. The Civil Rights Movement succeeded in many ways, which made the climate ripe for people with ideas outside the social norms to come forward. Feminists, gay rights campaigners, hippies and many other political movements together brought about changes in society, including changes for handicapped people.

Mom was born during The Depression, grew up during World War II, was married during the Korean War, was raising a family during the Vietnam War and grieved with the rest of the country at the assassination of the 35th president of the United States. She also witnessed much of the Civil Rights Movement, as well as the political movements of the 1960s

By the 1960s, society was more welcoming to handicapped people, and some accommodations were made, but it remained difficult for handicapped people to get around. Mom had no problems discussing those difficulties with whoever would listen.

Mom kept on doing all she could do, rather than depending on others to do everything for her. She said she could call on any one of the neighbors in Lincoln for help, but she rarely did. She had figured out ways to accomplish whatever needed to be done, and could do most things herself.

CHAPTER 8

Life in Minnesota

In 1966, the government shut down the air base in Lincoln. Arnold was transferred to the tower at Flying Cloud Airport in Eden Prairie, Minnesota. Gail and Arnold considered the opportunity seriously before taking the position. Moving to Minnesota would isolate them from both families, with the closest relatives more than six hours away in Racine, Wisconsin.

They decided to take the job as a step up the ladder for Arnold, planning to later find something closer to family. That was nearly fifty years ago, and Gail still lives in Minnesota.

It was January, when Arnold packed a few clothes in his car, along with other personal items, kissed his family good-bye and took off on the long drive north to the land of water and woods. Gail stayed in Lincoln so the children could finish the school year in familiar surroundings. The house also needed to be put on the market, and the family's belongings needed to be packed.

Located at the top of a bluff overlooking the Minnesota River bottoms, the breathtaking view from the Flying Cloud Airport included the city of Shakopee. The river bottoms vast water, bogs and trees separated the bluff from the city.

Arnold found a small yellow cabin to rent at the bottom of the hill, west of Flying Cloud, that included a small stove, kitchen sink and refrigerator, but it did not have a television. Being isolated from friends and family, he needed one. It was not long before he moved about a half-mile east to Sheer's Motel, where he had one large room, a bathroom and a television.

Arnold missed his family, and would travel to Lincoln as often as possible, making the long trip there and back in three days. Driving ten hours one way did not leave much time to spend with Gail and the girls, but he felt it was worth it.

Though living without Arnold was more difficult, Gail did well taking care of the girls and the house on her own, with a little help from the neighbors.

Selling the house proved to be a problem. The closing of the air base flooded the housing market with homes for sale. By the end of the summer, the house still had not sold. To make sure the girls started the school year in Minnesota, Gail and Arnold hired someone to manage the house while it was for sale, and Gail, the girls and the cat moved to Minnesota at the end of August. Most of their possessions were put in storage, and they stayed with Arnold at the motel.

Mr. and Mrs. Sheer, the motel owners, lived in an apartment on one end of the long brown single-level motel. Doors to motel rooms dotted the front of the building facing the parking lot, as well as the back of the building facing the woods. Arnold started with a room in the back, but moved to the front by the time the family arrived.

Poncho got into a tussle with the motel owner's cat, and ended up clawing the skin on Lucille's leg into shreds. Lucille had reached over Poncho to latch the screen door of the motel room so he would not burst through it. Concentrating so hard on the cat on the other side of the door, he did not realize it was Lucille reaching over him and he attacked. Afterwards, Poncho sulked about the room, seeming to be sorry for his actions.

Not knowing how long it would take to find a home, Gail and Arnold could not risk another attack on one of the girls. On the way to an appointment with a realtor, they took a detour to release Poncho into a corn field in the country. Because Poncho hunted in the fields near their home in Lincoln, Arnold felt he would survive in the corn field.

The appointment with the realtor, Lydia Haas, proved to be beneficial, not only in finding a house, but in finding a place to live in the meantime. Lydia, a powerful woman with dark hair and clear, confident eyes, owned an apartment building about five minutes from the motel at the east side of Chaska. She offered to rent the family a vacant basement apartment.

Within a week, Arnold and Gail moved the family from the motel room to the tiny apartment accessed by going down several stairs and walking through a narrow, crowded hallway. The apartment's low ceiling was held up by a beam in the living room on which Arnold kept hitting his head.

Soon after, Gail and Arnold found a three-bedroom rambler with a detached garage on Prairie Street, located within walking distance of the apartment. The little green house had a concrete porch with three stairs leading to the front door, and the back door was on the east side of the house near the garage.

Through the front door was the living room, with a hallway off to the right leading to the bathroom and bedrooms. Around to the left of the living room, was the door to the basement, and the dining room and kitchen were at the back of the house. One bedroom was on the west side of the kitchen, with a pocket door between the two and a door into the hallway. Lucille claimed that room. Gail and Arnold's bedroom was in the back right corner of the house, on the other side of Lucille's. Gail Arlene's was across the hall from theirs in the front corner of the house.

The full basement was unfinished, and the previous occupants had left an old upright piano, with intricate wood carvings and missing ivory on the keys. They felt it was too heavy to haul out of the basement. It still made decent music, and sitting in front of it, on Arnold's knee, was where Lucille and Gail Arlene learned how to play the piano.

The laundry room was installed in the basement, with a large wooden, claw-foot table placed in the corner next to the wash tubs for folding clothes. Arnold eventually set up a work shop in the back of the basement, and a family room was created opposite the laundry room.

The workshop supported many of Arnold's hobbies, including the creation of electrical equipment and toys. He built the family's first tube and resister color television from a kit and placed it on top of a small metal cupboard in the family room. Saturday nights were movie nights. Gail would get the girls bathed and rollers in their hair early in the evening, and the family would gather around the television. In front of that television was where Gail, Arnold and the girls watched the moon landing in 1969.

The climate change from a hotter, dryer Nebraska to a cooler, more humid Minnesota stimulated Gail's asthma, which the change in flora exacerbated. Frequent asthma attacks plagued her for many years, with at least one visit to the emergency room every spring.

When the family moved to Chaska, it was a small community of about 4,500 people. Everyone knew everyone, which at times, made it difficult on the newcomers. Several families in the neighborhood accepted newcomers, and one of Arnold's co-workers lived about two blocks west on the same street. Gail had no trouble making friends with a couple of the women in the neighborhood.

Lydia and her husband, Herb, took the Gail's family under their wings, and a lasting friendship developed. If she liked someone, Lydia had a kind heart and was an incredible friend, but if someone crossed her, she was a formidable adversary.

The girls started school at the Chaska public elementary at the top of the hill behind the neighborhood. No roads led directly to the school. When the bus picked up the girls, it would have to wind its way through the neighborhood and take the road up the hill on the west side. At the top, it would travel northeast to get to the school.

Gail set about making the house a home, and figuring out how to navigate around the area to take care of daily tasks. She had always been conscious of color combinations, and used whatever she had available to make the home environment as pleasing as possible.

Meals were never served out of a box or a pan. The table was always set, and even the infrequently used convenience foods were placed in serving dishes before they made it to the table. The family spent mealtimes together, sitting at the table, and the telephone rang unanswered during meals.

The whole neighborhood rarely did things as a group, but Gail and Arnold's friends frequently had barbeques, card parties and get togethers, which Gail enjoyed immensely. She loved social gatherings and enjoyed entertaining.

Several of the women, who were stay-at-home moms, gathered during the day. When the weather was nice, Gail often took the girls on walks to one of the other women's homes where she would sit and visit while Lucille and Gail Arlene played with the other children.

Lucille and Gail Arlene got along with most of the children in the neighborhood, but not all. As the newcomers, they were teased both in the neighborhood and at school, sometimes ruthlessly. Gail and Arnold did what they could do to shield them and provide a sense of security at home. They got into an argument with one of Lucille's teachers who insisted on calling Lucille by her first name, Ethel, which exacerbated the teasing. Students took the name and teased her by comparing Lucille to ethyl gasoline.

Sometimes other children would tease the girls by calling Gail names. Lucille had an argument with a girl who called Gail crippled. Lucille was adamant that her mother was not crippled, and angry that the girl could even think such a thing.

Tears streamed down her face as Lucille asked Gail if it was true. Gail told her it was true, and Lucille was crushed. Gail explained to her that everyone has some type of handicap; it is just that some people show it on the outside more than others.

Lucille sat on the curb in front of the house crying for what seemed like a long time, but what she learned she has carried with her for the rest of her life. Lucille said she learned to see people for who and what they are, and where their heart is, not what they look like or how they talk or walk.

"Because I have the mother I have, I have been able to experience so much more in my life. Handicaps of others don't get in the way of really knowing, and getting to know, others for who they are," said Lucille. "I am able to see people from the inside out, instead of the outside in, and I am not uncomfortable around people who have disabilities, as so many people are. I am able to get to the business of knowing them without the getting-used-to period that many people experience."

Gail and Arnold started bowling again, first joining a FAA league at the bowling alley at Southtown in Bloomington. They later joined leagues at the small bowling alleys in Chaska and Shakopee as well. For more than 30 years, they belonged to a couple's league, and each of them belonged to at least one other league.

Gail's Wednesday morning women's bowling team.

To make up for the fees paid for bowling, both Gail and Arnold became secretaries for different leagues. At one time, Gail was secretary for three leagues—one men's league and two women's leagues—and Arnold was secretary for a men's league. Gail got the job as the secretary for the men's league through the small eight-lane basement bowling alley on Fifth Street in Chaska. The owner suggested Gail when no one on the league wanted to take on the duties.

Those on the league were happy to have her, but Gail ran into problems when she went to the men's bowling association secretary's meetings. She was there representing sixteen to eighteen men, but the other secretaries would not let her vote because she was a woman. Some of them said that decision was unfair because she was representing the men in the league, but the majority said, "That will teach them to have a woman secretary."

"I didn't feel bad for me. I felt bad for the men," Gail said.

Gail also got involved with Christian Women's groups, which was where the seed was planted for her public speaking career to begin again. One never knows what a conversation with a stranger will do.

Gail had gone to a Christian Women's conference at the University of Minnesota in the Twin Cities, where a woman introduced herself. She had been watching Gail and was curious. They talked for a while, covering the usual ground of Gail's disability, how long she had cerebral palsy and how it had affected her life.

Out of the blue, Gail received a phone call from someone belonging to a group of people with various handicaps. Those in the group went to different organizations, schools, churches and clubs around the Twin Cities giving presentations to educate others about handicapped people. The caller heard about Gail from the woman at the conference, and invited her to join the group. She accepted the invitation, and began telling people her story.

It was while sharing her presentation that Gail found out about United Cerebral Palsy of Minnesota (UCP). Someone from UCP saw her presentation and asked her to become a member.

As a member of UCP, Gail gave presentations, volunteered at various events, worked on educating people about cerebral palsy and met many new people. She sat on the board of Gillette Children's Hospital as the UCP representative for three or four years, facilitated parent support groups, and participated in telethons to raise money for UCP.

In 1982, Gail produced the local portion of the national UCP telethon and invited Gail Arlene and her daughter to participate in a segment showing that cerebral palsy is not inherited.

Gail on stage during a telethon as one of the hosts
holds the microphone while Lucille sings.

Gail continued public speaking for years, telling her story at churches and organizations, long after she stopped working with UCP. She also was an advocate who pointed out changes that would make life easier for handicapped people.

The United States went through many growing pains and traumatic events in the 1970s. The turmoil of the previous decade's political movements continued as social and political norms were challenged. There was a growing disillusionment of government, a heightened concerned for the environment, and space exploration increased.

Student strikes protesting the Vietnam war temporarily closed 536 universities, high schools and colleges in 1970. President Richard Nixon, who resigned his presidency in 1974, negotiated a ceasefire with North Vietnam in 1973, diminishing the United States involvement in the war. North Vietnam captured Saigon in 1975, basically ending the war, and the north and south reunified the next year.

On the home front, the United States Congress guaranteed education access to the handicapped with the Education of All Handicapped Children Act of 1975. Gail was one of the fortunate children who grew up in an area where handicapped children were educated on the same level as everyone else. Not all children were as fortunate.

Another important decision made in the 1970s continues to affect children. In 1973, abortion was legalized through the court's decision in Roe vs. Wade. Legalizing abortion had a dramatic affect on society, both in its divisiveness and the number of children who were aborted. Both camps—pro-life and pro-abortion—lobbied extensively to convince the nation their ideas were correct.

For people like Gail, legalized abortion meant they could be robbed of the opportunity to live what could be a full life and be an inspiration to others. Gail had a conversation about that with Wayne, asking him if he would do it all again. She told him if she knew she was pregnant with a child like her, she would abort it.

"Honey, you can't do that," answered Wayne. "You can't break the chain of life."

After thinking about it, Gail decided he was right. She also began wondering where the line would be drawn. If babies with handicaps were aborted, or allowed to die, who would be next? Would medical treatment then be withheld from disabled adults, or old people? Who would make the decision who should live and who should die?

The Americans With Disabilities Act of 1990 made a difference for people like Gail. It was a wide-ranging civil rights law that prohibited, under certain circumstances, discrimination based on disabilities. It also forced public businesses and transportation services to make changes that gave handicapped people access to more places.

That was helpful, but often the decisions made about what constitutes handicap accessibility are made by people who are not handicapped without consulting those who are. Gail said accessibility is often made harder than it needs to be.

Gail has always looked for ways to accommodate handicaps and help others. Arnold was like that, too. He was always looking for ways to make life easier for Gail and to expand her life experiences. He was the one who came up with the idea of Gail driving a golf cart.

When Gail Arlene was about thirteen years old, the family moved from Prairie Street to the west end of Third Street, about a half-mile from downtown Chaska. The house was a large, gray tri-level home with two flights of about ten stairs each—one from the ground level to the kitchen, dining room and living room, and one from the living room to three bedrooms and a bathroom.

Arnold thought if Gail had a golf cart, she could get around easier by herself. The idea was a good one, but making it happen was a challenge. Arnold and Gail approached the city of Chaska about a permit to drive the golf cart on city streets as a handicapped vehicle, but the city ordinance did not have anything to address such a request.

It took several visits to city council meetings, a lot of discussion, and agreeing to a whole list of restrictions for Gail to get a permit. At one point, the city council was not going to allow her to cross U.S. Highway 212, which at the time ran through town parallel to the railroad tracks. Gail could get to most of what she needed on the south side of the highway, but the gas station, grocery store and church were located on the other side.

"We can't do that," said one council member. "It would defeat the purpose. She couldn't even go to the grocery store." The other council members relented, and permission was granted for Gail to cross the highway.

Arnold and Gail purchased a white golf cart with a windshield, a single bench seat and a small cargo spot in the back. Lights were added, and a large orange slow-moving-vehicle triangle was posted on the back. It also was rigged for left-handed driving, which Gail easily learned to do. The fact that a golf cart stopped when Gail removed her foot from the gas made Arnold more comfortable with the idea of her driving.

Though Gail was thankful that she could drive the golf cart in town, it always bothered her that children could ride their bicycles anywhere while the city restricted where she could go.

The new machine gave her more freedom and flexibility. After all the years of riding with Arnold, she could finally drive him around, but she had to remember to keep gas in the tank. Gail had driven Arnold to Crown of Glory Church, about half way up the hill off of Highway 41, and they ran out of gas. They called a friend who owned a gas station at the bottom of the hill. He laughed as he delivered the couple of gallons of gas. In his years of owning a station, it was the first time he had been called to bring gas for a golf cart.

Theodore, or Teddy for short, loved to ride on the golf cart, and he got excited any time Gail headed in its direction. Teddy was a half Pekinese and half German shepherd dog Gail received from Lydia a couple of years before. He would sit erect on the seat, next to Gail, his nose in the air as the wind blew through his long hair.

Lydia owned his Pekinese mother—which had a difficult time giving birth to the two large puppies—Teddy and his brother. Teddy was the shape of a large Pekinese, with the exception of the pug nose, and had much of the same coloring. His body was a little longer, and he had blonde hair mixed in with the long black and brown hair.

The day Gail was to bring Teddy home from Lydia's house, she had a hard time taking him. He climbed into Lydia's lap, put his front legs around her neck and cried like a baby.

"I can't do it," Gail said to Lydia. "I can't take him."

"You have to," said Lydia. She could not take care of three dogs.

So Gail took him home, and Teddy got so mad he nipped at her.

Arnold sat Teddy down like a child, pointed his finger at his nose admonishing him and said, "There will be no more of that. Do that one more time and out the door you go! I'm not going to have it!" Teddy understood. He never nipped at Gail again.

Arnold was never going to have any dogs in the house. He had grown to love cats, but he told Gail that cats and dogs could not live together. They had been married for about fifteen years before he allowed her to get her first puppy. The family was still living on Prairie Street, and already had a black cat with white paws named Boots. Gail and Arnold brought home a little black half-beagle, half-poodle puppy with soft curly hair, and Gail named her Dolly

Guests had brought dogs to visit before, and Boots would hibernate in the basement until they left. Dolly never left. After about a month of hibernating, Boots wanted to again join the family. She came upstairs, slapped Dolly on the nose and let her know who was boss.

The two never became friends, but they tolerated each other well. When Boots had kittens, Dolly, who never had puppies, adopted the kittens. Whenever they were out of the box the kittens shared with Boots, Dolly could cuddle them, play with them and act like their mother. But when they were in the box, Boots would not let Dolly near.

Dolly wandered off to die of old age shortly before Gail and Arnold got Teddy.

When Lucille and Gail Arlene were in high school, Arnold was put on a medical discharge from air traffic control. He had worked his way up to supervisor of the air traffic control tower, but the stress had taken its toll on his body. He was diagnosed with a spastic stomach and colon, and the medications he took meant he could no longer direct air traffic.

Rather than utilize Arnold's many years of knowledge by having him train new air traffic controllers, the government, in its infinite wisdom, put him out to pasture and offered to pay for schooling into another field. Three years later, after two back surgeries and taking two years of classes, he graduated from Northwestern Electronics Institute (NEI).

Though the schooling was paid for, lack of income depleted Gail and Arnold's savings. It took years for Arnold to move through the government's medical system and for it to acknowledge the stress of the job as the cause of his medical condition. He had worked with the government for more than 20 years, and after several years of jumping through hoops, he finally received a pension.

In December 1976, Arnold was recovering from back surgery when Lucille came home with her date, Joe Rief, on a Sunday night to tell Gail and Arnold they were going to be married on the next Friday. Lucille and Joe had dated about five years, much of the time through letters back and forth from Fort Bragg, North Carolina, where Joe was serving as a paratrooper in the Army.

Gail and Arnold were excited for Lucille, but Arnold would not be able to walk down the aisle to give away his daughter. Lucille asked Arnold's brother, John, if he would give her away.

The week at Gail and Arnold's home disappeared in a flurry of wedding preparations. Lucille's friend, Bernadine, made the wedding dress, Gail Arlene made the flowers, and arrangements were made for the wedding to take place at the Catholic Church on Second Street. Invitations were extended, and the groom's dinner set for Thursday night at Gail and Arnold's.

As the mother of the bride, Gail had no idea what she would wear to the wedding. She wore the same size tops and dresses as her two daughters, extending her options. She chose a floor-length dress belonging to Lucille, and Bernadine hemmed the dress as Gail was going out the door heading to the wedding.

Arnold stood at the window in the bathroom and watched the family leave the house, mourning that he was unable to walk his oldest daughter down the aisle.

After graduation from NEI, Arnold had a hard time finding a job, and a few years later, Gail and Arnold both took jobs at the Little Six Bingo Hall south of Shakopee, where Gail worked for about six years. As a bingo admissions clerk, Gail greeted people as they entered the hall and sold bingo packages. Her duties included opening a register when she arrived and closing out the drawer when she left.

Arnold started out doing the same thing, but he moved around. He later became a bingo caller, and then went over to the teepee, which was a small casino, where he did whatever needed to be done.

In the late 1970s, Lillie's health was deteriorating as her internal organs began to shut down. She had cirrhosis of the liver, though she was never a heavy drinker. She died in May 1980, a month before Gail Arlene's wedding.

Gail got a call in April letting her know her mother was dying, and had about two weeks to live. All of the family left Minnesota to be with her, Gail Arlene losing her job in the process, and Darlene left California to go home to Wichita.

Lillie was in the hospital, alert and glad to see everyone. The medical staff did all they could do to make her as comfortable as possible, and family members took turns staying at the hospital so she never had to be alone.

Lillie lived longer than the doctors expected. Gail and Arnold stayed at Lillie and Wayne's house, only going home to Minnesota when Arnold needed to meet with government doctors about his medical disability.

It was a hard time for Gail, and she spent every moment that she could with her mother. They talked about everything, including what would happen after Lillie died. Lillie had shared her treasures with certain people, creating special memories. She gave Gail specific instructions on whom to give those treasures.

"You have to write these things down," Gail told Lillie. "I won't remember." Lillie never wrote them down.

Though the hospital staff was wonderful, Lillie did not want to die there. She wanted to die at home, in the small house on the three-quarters-acre property her and Wayne purchased 25 years before. She had turned the property into an orchard, with a variety of fruit trees, and a garden of colorful flowers. She kept asking to go home.

Wayne ordered a hospital bed to be delivered and set up in the living room, after which Lillie was brought home. The spring air was comforting, and the May flowers were blooming. It was a wonderful time for Lillie to be on the property she loved so much.

The last thing Lillie saw was a bouquet of the flowers she had grown. Gail went out to the yard, cut a few flowers and put them in a vase for her. She died shortly after that, but family would not let her go. Darlene was hysterical, and Lillie came back, though she was in a coma. She moaned a mournful cry for about eight hours before she finally died, which was torture for Gail.

After Lillie died, Gail could not remember most of the things Lillie had told her, and Darlene was in shock. As the morticians took the body away, Gail Arlene gathered the clothes Lillie had chosen for her burial.

The funeral brought many of Lillie's numerous siblings and their children together with Wayne's family. The church was filled with people who loved Lillie and knew, without a doubt, where she had gone

Gail's relationship with Lillie was very close, and her death took its toll on her. She got angry with God for letting Lillie die, and stayed angry with him for more than a year.

The next decade was filled with Gail and Arnold trying to make ends meet. Arnold had developed a gambling problem, which cost him his job at Little Six. Since he took care of the family finances, Gail was unaware that the gambling monster had raised its head until it was too late.

To compound matters, the soft tissue in Arnold's neck was damaged in a major car accident. Gail and Arnold had been bowling at Southtown Bowling Alley and were headed home driving south on Interstate Highway 35W when a tire blew. The heavy traffic made it impossible for Arnold to limp the car to the right shoulder. He pulled the car off on the median as far as possible, where he and Gail waited for help.

The traffic kept moving past until a taxi plowed into the rear of their car. The driver had not been paying attention to the road and hit them at more than fifty-five miles per hour, crushing and spinning the car at the same time.

Traffic slowed, funneled to the far right and continued to limp past as emergency vehicles arrived on site. Lucille, who had been bowling with them, came upon the scene. She got out of her car and tried to get to her parents, but the police officers would not let her through to the accident. They told Lucille that her parents would be taken to a hospital in the Twin Cities, and she could meet them there.

The officers gave Lucille the wrong information. When she got to the hospital, she found out Gail and Arnold were being taken to St. Francis Hospital in Shakopee. Lucille called Gail Arlene, who raced to St. Francis. Gail had small cuts all over her face where broken glass had pierced her skin. Her body was bruised and thrown out of whack.

Arnold, on the other hand, had to be cut out of the car. The drivers seat had broken, which plunged him into a prone position. The soft tissue in his neck was damaged to the point where he was unable to hold his head up straight, which added to his health problems. He never fully recovered from the accident, and then he got emphysema from smoking most of his life.

With his health issues and his age, finding a job got even more difficult. They lived on Arnold's pension, which was not enough to pay for living expenses and the mountain of debt.

They lost the house on Third Street in Chaska, which necessitated a move. Their church family helped get the house cleaned up and move all their possessions to the new home, a small rambler with a basement on Marshall Road in Shakopee. It had an attached garage, a large fenced-in yard, and most everything Gail needed for daily tasks on the main level.

Gail lost her job at Little Six because of discrepancy between her packages and the till. There was a last minute rush of customers, and one of them wanted to change a bingo package to a different one, which Gail no longer had. She refunded the original package cost, but the customer took it with when trying to find a different package.

Now both Gail and her husband were without work. Searching for work at the unemployment office, Gail ran across an advertisement seeking interpreters at Murphy's Landing, an eighty-eight-acre historical village along the Minnesota River. Given her knowledge and interest in history, Gail applied. She received a call requesting that she come in to talk about being a volunteer, but Gail did not want to volunteer. She needed a job, not a hobby.

Having already planned on visiting Wayne in Kansas, Gail left the state without calling back. When she came home, Arnold told her someone from the Landing had called several times while she was gone.

"Maybe you should volunteer," Arnold told Gail. "It may lead to a job."

Gail still did not want to volunteer. She needed the money, and knew her experience working with telethons was worth more than a volunteer. She called and agreed to a meeting with Deanna, interpreter coordinator at Murphy's Landing.

"There's something you should know," Gail told Deanna when they met. "I have an attitude problem."

"What is that?"

"If I'm good enough to volunteer, I'm good enough to get paid."

They talked for a while, and then Deanna took Gail on a walk from the offices to the town square, which had a park in the middle with three buildings lining the dirt road on the west and three on the east. They headed to the Tabaka House at the northeast corner of the square, next to the overlook of the Minnesota River constructed by the Works Progress Administration (WPA) in the 1930s. The house was the newest in the village, constructed around 1890, and was interpreted as the mayor's house.

The gray house came with all the fixings, including a large front porch. The interpreter that day was a man who Gail thought did a lousy job. She told Deanna she was appalled at the way the he was interpreting the house.

"You think you could do better?" Deanna asked.

"I know I could!"

Deanna wanted to hire Gail, but her boss was sure Gail was too shy and would never make a good interpreter.

"You'll be sorry if you let this one go," Deanna said. "She will be good."

Deanna finally got her boss to agree to hiring Gail for a paid trial period. Her first two assignments were to interpret the Tabaka House and the Atwater House. The Atwater house was in the middle on the opposite side of the town square.

Gail passed the trial period and was hired on full time. She worked for about nine years as an interpreter, mostly in the Mayor's house. She used the opportunity to not only educate people about history, but her persona as the mayor's wife gave her a lead into telling people about how handicapped people were treated in the past.

Most people with handicaps were hidden in the 19th century. When company came, they were kept in a bedroom or taken outside. A handicapped child was considered a weakness of the father, and many handicapped children were mistreated.

"I was one of the lucky ones," Gail would tell the visitors. "I was even educated until the sixth grade!"

When she played a maid, she would tell the visitors she was lucky to have a job because most handicapped people were not given the opportunity to work.

Gail tried on different personas, seeking one that would fit best. Many of the stories she shared with the visitors were stories of things that actually happened to her grandmothers. The persona that stuck for the longest was Mother Loomis, the mayor's wife. Being married to the mayor and the hostess to guests was a big deal, and she played it up well.

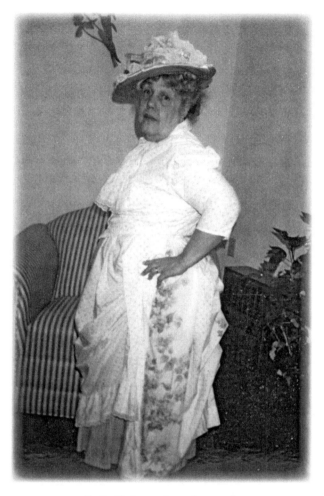

Gail all dressed up for work.

Gail always walked with a limp, sometimes dragging her right toes. She did not always have the strength and control in the ankle to keep the toes from dragging. The uneven terrain at the Landing made it difficult to get from one place to another without falling. Though she did well, there were occasional falls. Once in a while, she would catch a ride on the trolley from the office to the house.

One Sunday, Gail was so tired she interpreted the entire house from a chair stationed in the center near the dining room. A woman came back a few days later saying she just had to hear Gail's spiel again. She was surprised when Gail walked her through the house, instead of interpreting from the chair.

Gail's time at Murphy's Landing allowed her to act, and she was able to blend that with her other interest—history.

Four grandchildren were born born by 1986, enlarging the family and capturing the hearts of Gail and Arnold. Spending time and sharing experiences with the grandchildren were precious, and they gave the grandchildren the opportunity to spend time with Gail at the Landing.

While in high school, Gail's granddaughter, Joy, spent a summer living with Gail while she worked with an acting group from Gustavus Adolphus College. Every year the college hired actors to perform throughout the summer. It also auditioned for interns to perform one day a week to give the actors a break. The interns would be at the Landing all week with the actors, and perform on Tuesdays on the stage in the town hall. The interns also performed random poetry recitals around the site and interacted with the guests.

Knowing Joy's interest in acting, Gail told her about the program. Joy auditioned and was selected as one of the four interns.

"When we weren't performing, it felt as if we spent time living in the 1800s," said Joy. "We would play croquet and checkers, and I remember many lunches that Grandma and I would have next door with Lynn, who cooked wonderful food using the old 1800s stove."

The general store, located two buildings down from the Tobaka house, served as the home base for the acting interns and the proprietor was their supervisor. Joy thought it would be fun to start a mail system throughout the Landing, giving interpreters a way to communicate throughout the day. The general store also became the post office, and the interns served as the mailmen. Though writing letters was a slow, challenging project for Gail, she supported Joy's venture by creating mail.

Gail's grandson, Mat, also spent a week with her at the Landing, apprenticing at the blacksmith shop during the day. He made a knife blade that Arnold took to the cobbler to create a handle. When Mat got it back, it had a wood handle and a leather sheath.

The other grandchildren visited the Landing on a regular basis. Having children around was part of a living museum. When a young Spencer, dressed in 1800s garments, chased a cat through the kitchen as Gail was talking to visitors, it added authenticity to the interpretation.

Gail's granddaughter, Robin, absorbed information like a sponge. She was able to interpret the dress maker's shop by the time she was ten years old. Gail gave her grandchildren the opportunity to learn about history in a personal way, by volunteering to live as people did in the 1800s.

Even with all the problems, Gail and Arnold took in strays, both animals and people. Lucille brought home an eighteen-year-old friend, Karen Dobbs, who had lost both parents—her dad when she was two years old and her mom when she was fifteen years old. Gail and Arnold took Karen into their hearts, and she never left. She joined the family as one of their daughters.

Gail and Arnold taught their girls to see the value of family, and changed the idea of family from "common ancestors" to "mutual love and respect."

As walking got harder for Gail, she fell more often. Arnold's health also had been failing, and they decided it was time to get a set of electric scooters, which would give them both more mobility. Arnold was looking forward to being able to take walks again with Gail.

Arnold died in 1994, a week before the scooters were ready, and Gail was afraid she could not survive on her own. She had gone from her father's house, to a dormitory, to her husband's home. Arnold had been doing the little things that were hard for her, like tying her shoes. Who would do them now?

There was no money, only thirty dollars cash in the cupboard. Arnold had life insurance, but it would be about six to eight weeks before the money would make its way to Gail. She knew the mortician, and he agreed do the funeral and let her pay later.

Gail would be receiving a survivors' pension from the federal government, but that also would take time for the paperwork to be processed. Her small paycheck, plus the thirty dollars cash, would not be enough for her to live on while everything was stalled in red tape.

For the first time in her life, Gail went to the county Social Services office to request emergency help to purchase food. The woman sitting behind the desk looked at her with disdain. She treated Gail as if everything she said was a lie, and made an already unbearable grieving process worse. At the end of the traumatic encounter, Gail received about $200 emergency help, with the stipulation that she would pay it back.

Gail lived alone for a couple of years in the duplex she and Arnold had been renting, before moving into an independent-living senior apartment building. She changed her shoes from laces to velcro, and later got a brace to hold her right foot in position so the toes would not drag. That brace cut down on the frequency of her falls.

The scooter opened up a whole new world. It made it possible for Gail to touch the ocean waves for the first time, and climb mountain paths by herself. It made it possible for her to go more places and see more things.

Gail found ways to get where she needed to go, eventually purchasing a handicap van so others could drive her without the hassle of her trying to get in and out of a car.

When she moved into the senior apartment building, Gail quit working at Murphy's Landing. The uneven terrain of the gravel roads and walkways throughout the Landing made it difficult for her to walk without falling.

She began to channel her energies in other directions. First, Gail challenged the management at the apartment building because it did not want her cat. She argued that management could not require seniors to give up their pets to live in subsidized independent apartments, and ended up winning.

The apartment Gail rented was a handicapped apartment, with wider doors, lower cupboards and a shower nearly the same level as the bathroom floor. It also had a pull cord by the bed and in the bathroom.

Gail started playing cards with others in the building, volunteering at the adjacent nursing home and reading stories to children at the library.

Many of the residents went back and forth between the nursing home and the apartment building, but the doors between were not automatic. Gail spoke up, saying that the doors were difficult to use for many of the residents. That led to handicapped buttons and keypads that automatically open the doors.

Many things around the complex—which now includes an assisted living wing and a memory care wing—changed because Gail was not afraid to speak up.

Joy and Gail in their seventies.

In 1999, Gail flew out to California to spend some time with Darlene. Wayne had moved out there about ten years previous because of his deteriorating physical condition. Twelve different kinds of arthritis were ravaging his body and moving around became difficult. Darlene and her husband, Cliff, welcomed Wayne into their home and took care of him.

By the time Gail stepped on the plane for that October 1999 visit, Wayne's care had become too much for Darlene and Cliff to handle. He had been transferred to a nursing home, and Cliff had been moved to a memory care unit because of Alzheimer's disease.

When Gail stepped off the plane, Darlene was not at the airport to greet her and there was no answer when Gail called the house. She called a friend and asked to be taken to Darlene's home in Riverside. Gail and her friend found Darlene's lifeless body curled up on the bed clutching a pillow to her heart. She was buried in California.

A little more than a year later, Wayne died. His body was shipped back to Wichita where he was buried next to Lillie.

∾

It has been several years since Mom turned in her scooter for an electric wheelchair, and at 81, does not walk anymore. She takes a step or two when she is transferring from the chair to the bed or toilet, but her legs have basically quit working.

Her lungs also have deteriorated from the many years of asthma and second-hand smoke. She wears oxygen when she is sleeping, and a cold can put her in the hospital.

Mom moved into the assisted living wing of the complex and has people who comes to her apartment every day to help her shower, get dressed, be there when she is transferring and help her get ready for bed. She has a small kitchen in her apartment, but meals are served in a community dining room.

Mom continues to astound people with the way she does everyday things able-bodied people take for granted, like getting into bed. Years ago, she figured out that satin sheets would make it easier for her to move in bed, so now she wears satin pajamas and slides in on satin sheets. She puts her wheelchair close to the bed, sits on the edge of the bed, and lies back, using her foot to push on the wheelchair, sliding her into the bed. She also has a bar on each side of the bed so she can use her left arm to help her turn.

Even with the adaptations, getting into bed is hard, and it takes a long time, as do dressing and undressing. As she gets older, everything takes more time than it used to, but Mom never ceases to find ways to do things. Though her body is fighting her, she does not give up.

People seem surprised when Mom shows up at events around town by herself. They often ask her if she is alone, as if she always needs someone with her because she is in a wheelchair.

"People see the wheelchair as a disability," said Mom. "I see it as an ability."

Mom is in the first generation of people to be helped with surgeries and therapy. The doctors did not know what aging would do, and her body still confounds them at times. She was told she would be in a wheelchair full time by the time she was 50 years old.

As always, she showed them.

EPILOGUE

Mom's life has been an inspiration to many, though I didn't understand that until I was thirteen years old. I had heard her story various times, accompanying her at different speaking engagements. To me, it seemed ordinary. Because she is my mother, her story is my story.

We were at a mother-daughter banquet at a church. I participated in the fashion show right before the guest speaker, who happened to be Mom. As I sat on the floor by the door in the back of the sanctuary, I watched the faces of those in the audience, glued to every word she was saying. Some eyes were glistening with tears. Normally antsy youngsters were still. That is when I realized her life truly is a miracle.

There are many more stories and anecdotes about Mom's strong will, perseverance and audacity. But this book was not written to tell you everything. It was written to help you see the odds that one person beat to live a long full life, and realize everyone has something to overcome. Here is an example to prove that overcoming obstacles is possible. If you can keep moving forward, not only is it possible, it is probable.

Mom overcame many adversities with a substandard body, and she advocated for human dignity and the rights of everyone. What better model could one have grown up with?

Her life has taught me many things:

- ✿ God presents us with many opportunities in what we may label "coincidences." Look for what He is doing in your life, and let Him be your peace.

- ✿ You never know what someone is going through or where he or she has been. We sit here judging people and asking why they do not do more, yet it may be a struggle for them just to get out of a bed.

- ✿ Just because a body is broken does not mean there is not an intelligent, charming, fun person in there. "You don't throw away a present just because the package is broken," Mom would say.

- ✿ See the blessings of every day, rather than search for what is wrong. There are blessings in every minute. We just have to stop long enough to see them.

- ✿ Keep moving forward, though it may be one baby step at a time. If something is important, you can do it.

- ✿ Nothing, and I mean nothing, comes close to the value of family and friends. If money, jobs and material possessions are more valuable than the people in your life, happiness eludes you.

- ✿ And finally: There is NO TIME TO QUIT!

CPSIA information can be obtained at www.ICGtesting.com
Printed in the USA
BVOW04s1603190214

345422BV00001B/3/P